101 THINGS SMART GIRLS DO

101 THINGS SMART GIRLS DO

A Teen Girl's Guide to Becoming Fearless, Resilient, and Unstoppable

RACHEL SPADE

Illustrations by Brianna Dandurand

Published by Pudding Lane Press
Second Edition 2024
ISBN 978-0-6456687-9-7

For all the girls out there,
quietly gathering their strength,
waiting for their moment to shine.

Contents

Ignite Your Spark!

Empowering Yourself for a Brighter Future

Have you ever wondered what you could achieve if you didn't let fears or doubts hold you back? What brilliant ideas would you bring into this world? What brave risks would you joyfully take to create the life you dream about?

Stop and think about that for a minute. Really, let those thoughts sink in. Because they're not just hypothetical questions—living with total self-belief, resilience, and courage is totally possible for you.

That's the power of embracing the smart girl mindset.

Now, don't let this book's title mislead you—being a "smart girl" isn't about getting good grades, although that's certainly an admirable goal. It's about making smart choices that empower you, and help you grow, progress, and ultimately live your best life.

Smart girls approach life with curiosity, grit, and a willingness to learn and adapt. They think for themselves instead of just following the crowd. They know that fear and self-doubt are obstacles to be overcome, not limitations to be accepted.

Now is the perfect time to cultivate a smart girl mindset.

Your teen years are a period of intense growth, big emotions, and deep questions about who you are and what you value. They're a time of fearless dreaming and redefining what you thought you knew about yourself. Why not harness the momentum of these formative years to start getting seriously smart?

So, the obvious question is: *What do smart girls do?*

That's why I wrote this book—to be your guide. In the following pages, we'll explore 101 powerful strategies that will equip you with the tools to become a fearless, resilient, and unstoppable smart girl—strategies I wish someone had shared with me when I was your age.

We'll look at how to rewire your brain for a growth mindset, ditch the toxic comparison game, tune into your intuition, prioritize self-care, communicate your needs effectively, and much more. Because you have incredible power to shape your own reality and create an amazing life, however you define that for yourself.

My role is simply to encourage you and help you develop these invaluable skills that will serve you for the rest of your life—skills that will empower you to become the extraordinary young woman you are destined to be.

So get comfy, take a deep breath, and let's start this journey together!

Be Brilliant, Be You

Unleashing Your Inner Awesome

"Are you even braving the unknown if you don't have self-doubt?" asked Mrs. Davey. She was my homeroom teacher. Her voice was friendly, but her gaze was sharp. Her question caught me off guard, and I couldn't help but feel a little defensive. Was she suggesting that I didn't have what it takes to be courageous?

I must have looked bewildered because she laughed and continued: "It's a sign that you're doing something outside your comfort zone. It's proof of your courage. Proof that you are going somewhere you haven't been before; proof that you are being you—everything you are supposed to be."

She made a point, and a marvelous one, for that matter. I had always considered self-doubt a weakness, a character stain I desperately needed to wash out. But she was making me see it in a refreshing new light. Perhaps self-doubt was a necessary part of growth. Maybe it was a sign that I was pushing myself to be better.

I must have looked lost in thought because after a moment she nudged me and asked, "Hey, are you alright?"

I nodded, still thinking about her words. "I'm just... I don't know. I've never really thought about it that way before."

She smiled the kindest smile I've ever seen. "Well, that's the beauty of living. There's always something new to discover. Something new to learn. So long as you stay true to yourself and keep pushing, you'll find your way alright."

Something about the way she spoke to me made me feel like she knew exactly what she was talking about. Maybe it was the crinkles around her eyes that suggested wisdom and a lifetime of experience or the quiet echo of confidence radiating from the sound of her words. Either way, I was grateful for her perspective. It was easy to get caught up in the comparison net, worrying too much about what other people thought of me. Mrs. Davey was reminding me that I was enough, just as I was.

"Thanks for the pep-talk," I said as I headed to first period. "It makes me feel a little better about... you know, everything."

"It was my pleasure. Remember: Be brilliant, be you."

Since that day, those words have clung to me like a second layer of skin, refusing to let go, even as time passed. So now, let me pass those words on to you. It's time to unleash your inner awesomeness and show the world just how brilliantly you can shine.

1. Be Unapologetically You

Have you ever stopped to think about how many people there are in the world, yet nobody talks exactly like you, laughs like you, or loves like you? All of us are truly one of a kind. Think about how dull and uneventful life would be if we were all the same; if we all thought the same or dressed the same. It sounds pretty boring, doesn't it? That's because it is!

So, celebrate all the wonderful things that make you unique. Maybe you're a pretty cool guitar player or have a special knack for drawing. Or perhaps you're a great listener or someone who isn't afraid to speak their mind.

Whatever it is, always remember that your uniqueness is your strength, and your individuality is your superpower. Embrace your quirks, dreams, and talents, for they are the special sauce that makes you you.

Know, too, that when you appreciate your uniqueness and the uniqueness of others, you help create a world that's diverse, exciting, and filled with the rich tapestry of humanity. So, take a breath and be unapologetically you because the world is a better place with your voice and perspective in it.

2. Discover Your Passions

One of the advantages of being a teenager is that you have your whole life ahead of you, filled with endless possibilities waiting to be discovered. So, how you choose to spend your precious time and where you focus your energy matters. Will you settle for the ordinary, a life of simply going with the flow and following the crowd? Or do you aspire to wake up each day with boundless enthusiasm because you're following your heart and doing what you love?

If the latter sounds more appealing to you, then discovering what you're passionate about is the first step on this exciting journey. Your passions are the sparks that ignite your true potential.

Nothing beats the sheer joy of knowing what you want out of life and being unafraid to go after it. That clarity can give you a much-needed confidence boost and help to motivate you to keep on going when faced with challenges.

So how do you find what your passions are? Well, I've just the tips to help you find them:

- **Try something new.** There is a novelty in newness. That's a motto I particularly love. Do you find yourself doing the same old thing every day? How about you break out of that routine and do something you rarely do? Sign up for that coding course you've been reading about online or that dance class your friend told you about. Join a sports team or volunteer in your community. You never know what might spark your interest and lead you down a path of passion.
- **Pay attention to what excites you.** When was the last time your heart raced? When was the last time you looked forward to doing something? When you find the image of that memory, think about what you were doing. Perhaps you get a thrill from being up on stage or writing stories meant to inspire, or maybe

solving complex equations or working with numbers gets you really excited. Pay attention to those moments and try to incorporate some of those things into your daily routine.

- **Explore the world online.** Consider yourself so incredibly lucky for being born into this era. You have so much information at your fingertips that's begging to be explored. Join online communities related to your interests, follow people on social media who inspire you, and seek out blog posts and podcasts on topics you're curious about. Who knows? In just a while, you might be starting a new and exciting podcast of your own.
- **Seek out inspiration in the world around you.** Take a step outdoors and let the beauty of nature inspire you. Visit your local library and lose yourself in the pages of a good book, exploring different worlds and perspectives. Or, put your headphones on and try listening to a different playlist each week.

Your passions are waiting to be found. All you need to do is put yourself out there and look for them. If you need some more inspiration, take a moment to read about these teens who were unafraid to go after their interests and passions:

- **Shubham Banerjee** taught himself how to build a braille printer out of LEGOs at just 13-years old. He went on to start his own company, Braigo Labs, with the goal of making braille printing accessible for everyone.
- **Gitanjali Rao** is a teenager who developed a device to detect lead in drinking water and won the 2017 Discovery Young Scientists Award!
- **Alina Morse** from Michigan started her own healthy candy company, Zollipops, at the age of seven and is now a successful entrepreneur with her product sold in stores nationwide.

(P.S.: Your passion doesn't have to be big for it to matter. If it means something to you, it matters, alright?)

3. Know What You Stand For

Growing up, my mother was always dropping little nuggets of wisdom on me. From *"always wear sunscreen"* to *"if you can't say anything nice, don't say anything at all."* She always seemed to know just what to say to make me feel more prepared for the world outside.

One phrase that has stuck with me over the years is, *"You cannot go about life not knowing who you are or what you stand for."* I don't think I knew what it meant at that time. I was a kid, after all, with no real sense of self outside of what my peers thought of me.

It wasn't until my teenage years that her words really stuck with me. As I began to form my own beliefs and opinions, I realized that knowing who I was and what I stood for was crucial. Without that foundation, I was pretty much like a ship without a rudder—easily swayed by the opinions of others.

Knowing what you stand for is all about understanding your values and beliefs. They are the guiding principles that shape your thoughts, actions, and decisions in life, providing a moral compass to help you navigate through the complexities of the world.

Sometimes, figuring out what you stand for can be tough, and that's totally okay! It takes time and self-reflection. So, start by asking yourself questions like, "What makes me happy? What makes me angry? What do I care about deeply?" Your answers can give you clues about what your values and beliefs may be.

If you need a little help, look at the value and belief statements on the following page and see if any resonate with you. Remember, there are no wrong answers, only what's right for you.

Values	Beliefs
Integrity	Everyone deserves to be treated with respect.
Respect	Hard work is what leads to success.
Loyalty	Family is a very important aspect of life.
Courage	True happiness is something that comes from within.
Reliability	Positive thinking has the power to influence the outcome.
Creativity	Honesty is always the best policy, regardless of how hard it is.
Kindness	We must take care of our environment as best we can.
Patience	Equality is something that should apply to everyone.
Gratitude	Health and well-being must be prioritized so that you can live the best life possible.
Trustworthiness	Kindness and empathy make the world a better place.

When you know what you stand for, it's easier to make choices that align with your true self. You won't feel pressured to do things just because everyone else is doing them. Instead, you'll be confident in your decisions, even when faced with challenges. Now, doesn't that sound like a great place to be?

4. Value Your Thoughts and Opinions

Your thoughts and opinions are like your personal treasure chest filled with gems. They are precious and valuable, so it's important you treat them with the respect they deserve. Now, I know that in this digital age, it can be tempting to look for validation from others on what to think or feel. But let me tell you, it's okay to stand firm in what you believe. Don't be afraid to speak up and share your thoughts with others.

Here are some ways to better understand your thoughts and opinions and build your confidence in expressing them.

- **Ask yourself why, and do it more often.** Why do you feel the way you do about certain things? Regularly questioning yourself in this way can lead to deeper self-awareness and a better understanding of your perspective. It's like peeling back the layers of an onion to discover the core of your thoughts and emotions.
- **Do your research.** The more you know about a subject, the more confident you'll feel in standing up for it. And always remember, it's okay to change your mind.
- **Trust your instincts.** The gut is sometimes a valuable indicator of whether or not you're making the right decision. Trusting that you know what's best and right for you will help you develop a stronger sense of trust in your opinions.

On the flip side, it's important to respect the thoughts and opinions of others as well. Chances are, you won't always agree with the people around you—that's just life. But by listening to and respecting the ideas of others, you'll be able to have a deeper, more meaningful conversation that can lead to new insights and ideas. Pretty cool, isn't it?

5. Be Brave

Bravery, in its purest form, is the audacious act of venturing down the road less traveled. It means having the courage to be your true self in a world that sometimes pressures you to conform. It's about facing challenges head-on, whether big or small and believing in your ability to overcome them.

It's perfectly natural to feel a racing heart or sweaty palms when faced with the unknown. Whether standing up in front of the class to read a poem, confronting a bully, pursuing your passions, or daring to dream big, bravery comes into play. Every time you take that bold step, you challenge yourself to grow, learn, and break free from limitations.

Even in the smallest acts of bravery, like admitting a mistake, apologizing to a friend, or trying something new, you build resilience.

So, next time your heart flutters with trepidation, put on your invisible cape and remember that being brave is not the absence of fear but the triumph over it. When you embrace your bravery, you unlock your true potential.

6. Believe in Yourself

When I was younger, I remember thinking I could do anything. Back then, I had dreams of singing and performing on stage. Yet, during my teenage years, doubt slowly crept in. Other people's opinions began to cast shadows on my self-belief and confidence. I abandoned the piano and left the school choir behind. It wasn't until my adult years that I rediscovered my love for music. I started taking piano lessons again, began writing songs, and realized I had a talent worth embracing.

During your teenage years, it can be easy to be swayed by those around you. A hurtful comment hurled in the school playground or a dismissive look from a so-called friend can derail you from chasing your dreams. That's why it's so important to surround yourself with people who uplift, support, and encourage you.

On the days when you feel anxious or unsure—because there will be those days—and you feel self-doubt begin to settle over you like a dark cloud, remember that it's okay not to have all the answers right now. Life is a journey of learning and growing. Embrace each challenge as an opportunity to learn and each setback as a stepping stone to success.

So, believe me when I tell you that believing in yourself, your worth, your talents, and your dreams is more important than what anybody else thinks of you. When you do, you'll possess the power to overcome obstacles, no matter how daunting they may seem, and shine like the star you are meant to be!

And as we come to the close of this chapter, I want to remind you that your best days are still ahead of you. Your happiest days are ahead of you. Your most beautiful days are ahead of you. Keep yourself and your heart open to all that is coming and to all you already have. And when all those things you've been working toward come your way, know that you are forever worthy of every single one of them.

Riding the Rollercoaster

Navigating Your Emotions and Feelings

You know those days when everything feels out of control? Or you think the universe has a diabolical plan to make your life miserable? Your hair won't cooperate, homework is piling up, and your crush hasn't texted back in hours. We've all been there. On days like that, it can be hard to figure out what you really want or need. So, you might turn to your heart and ask it to speak up.

But your heart isn't always clear with its answers. Sometimes it whispers gently. Other times, it roars like a stormy ocean, overwhelming you. And sometimes, it's silent. So, what do you do then? You could try a different approach. Ask your gut instead of your heart. Do you know that feeling in your stomach when something feels right (or very wrong)? That's your gut talking. And, unlike your heart, it's usually pretty direct.

Of course, it's not foolproof. Sometimes, even your gut might feel conflicted, but that's okay. Emotions are tricky, and no one has all the answers. On those endless question mark days, close your eyes, take a deep breath, and listen. You might not always get a clear answer, but sometimes, giving yourself a moment of calm can help you find your way.

7. Embrace Your Emotions

No emotion is bad. There's enough space for joy to exist alongside sadness, frustration, and disappointment. There's enough space for hope to exist alongside all the uncertainties, too.

It's important to remember that we all have a wide range of emotions, and it's okay to feel them all, even the not-so-pleasant ones. It's easy to get caught up in the idea that you should always be happy, but the reality is it's perfectly natural to feel anger, loneliness, and confusion at times. These emotions might not feel good, but they serve an important purpose. They help you navigate the ups and downs of life and learn from your experiences. Without these emotions, life would be a lot less meaningful.

But here's the thing: These emotions don't have to take over your life. It's all about creating space for all your positive and negative emotions. This means acknowledging, processing, and using them as a tool for growth. When you're in the midst of a difficult emotion, it can feel like it will last forever. But the reality is that your emotions are like waves—they come and go. You can ride out the tough ones and appreciate the good ones when they come. So how do you embrace the fullness of your emotions?

- **Pay attention.** You can start by paying attention to how your emotions influence your thoughts and actions. Notice patterns in your behavior and the triggers that lead to specific emotions. For example, if you tend to get anxious before exams, try to identify the thoughts that contribute to your anxiety. By being aware of these patterns, you can better manage your response.
- **Notice and name your feelings.** How do you feel when certain things happen? When you can pinpoint what that emotion is, say it out loud to yourself. You might feel proud when something happens, or you might feel a little sad or even nervous before something like a big competition.

- **Reflect, but don't ruminate.** Reflecting on the negatives is just as important as reflecting on the positive side of things. Understanding why you may sometimes feel negative will help you become a more well-rounded individual—someone who can deal with the negatives in the future. It's all about finding a healthy balance and using your reflections to move forward and make positive changes.
- **Learn to manage your emotions healthily.** Take deep breaths, count to 10, and remove yourself from a situation temporarily if you're feeling overwhelmed. Engaging in activities like mindfulness or meditation can also help you develop a sense of calmness and self-control.
- **Work on focusing on one emotion.** Choose an emotion. It could be anything from joy, sadness, or irritation, and tell yourself that you're going to track that emotion for the whole day. Notice what triggers that emotion and how you respond when it comes up. By doing so, you can start to identify patterns and recognize areas where you may want to work on improving your emotional regulation.

8. Practice Self-Awareness

Self-awareness is your ability to recognize and understand your character, as well as all your different moods and their effect on others and yourself. It equips you with an honest evaluation of your strengths and weaknesses, enabling you to identify areas that require more focus. Let's go over some practices that make this work.

- **Learn to look at yourself objectively.** Try to see yourself as if you were looking at someone else. Take a step back and observe your thoughts, actions, and behavior without judgment. It's not about being overly critical or harsh but about being curious and open-minded.
- **Give yourself a time-out.** Find a quiet space where you can have some alone time. Take a deep breath and try to clear your mind. This will help you create a mental space for self-reflection.
- **Think about recent situations or events that made you feel a particular way.** Ask yourself questions like "Why did I react that way?" or "What were the thoughts and emotions behind my actions?" This will help you dig deeper into your motivations and feelings.
- **Imagine how someone else might see the situation.** What would they think or feel? This will help you better understand the situation and your role in it.
- **Ask for honest feedback from people you trust, like friends, family, or mentors.** Sometimes, others can see things about you that you might overlook yourself.
- **Don't ignore your triggers.** Self-aware people can recognize their emotions as they occur. It's important that you remain flexible and adapt to your situation. Don't deny your emotions space to exist in; don't be too rigid with them.

9. Write Your Thoughts Down

Have you ever felt like your head is about to explode with all the thoughts and emotions running around in there? Well, writing them down can be a total lifesaver! Seriously, it's like getting everything out of your mind and onto paper. It makes it so much easier to understand what you're feeling and why. And the best part? It can help you make positive changes in your life by identifying patterns in your thoughts and actions. Plus, journaling can be an awesome way to grow as a person and reflect on yourself. So why not give it a try? You might be surprised at how much it helps.

Journal prompts for self-reflection

It can be a bit of a challenge to figure out all that you want to say and write about when journaling. So, to take a little bit of the stress away from the process, here are some journal prompts to help you get started.

- What are the things that make you feel the most calm?
- How can you encourage yourself to avoid getting discouraged or demotivated when you're trying something new?
- How are you embracing your most authentic self, even if it looks slightly different from what others deem or find acceptable?
- When do you feel happiest in your skin?
- Write three things that you love about yourself and explain why.
- What makes you unique, and how can you use more of this uniqueness?
- What dream of yours do you wish would come true?
- Name a moment in your life you're most proud of.

As you write and learn more about yourself, don't worry about getting the perfect answer. This is a practice for you and you alone. That's all that matters.

10. Express Your Emotions in a Healthy Way

Emotional expression is the process of communicating your feelings to others through your body language, tone of voice, and facial expressions. It's a way of conveying your inner state to others and plays a crucial role in building and maintaining healthy relationships.

Think about a time when you met someone who was difficult to read. Maybe they spoke in a monotone voice and had a neutral expression on their face. It can be challenging to understand how they're feeling or what they're trying to communicate. In contrast, when someone is expressive about their emotions, it can help you to feel more connected to them and understand their perspective.

Here's an example: You may have a friend who always seems happy and upbeat. They greet you with a smile and seem energetic when you're around them. But one day, you notice they seem upset, and they're not smiling like they usually do. When you ask them what's wrong, they open up to you and share that they're struggling with something that's been weighing on them. Without their emotional expression, you wouldn't have known that something was bothering them, and you wouldn't have been able to offer support.

Emotional expression matters because it helps you to connect with others on a deeper level and build meaningful relationships. When you're open and honest about your feelings, it allows others to see you as you truly are. This can lead to greater trust and empathy, as others can relate to your experiences and emotions.

Here are some ways to help you express your emotions.

- **Be present.** Develop the habit of being present in the moment. Mindfulness exercises, such as focusing on your breath or observing your thoughts without judgment, can help you become more aware of your emotions and express them in a healthy way.
- **Get creative!** Engage in activities such as painting, drawing, writing, or playing a musical instrument. These outlets can provide a means of expressing your emotions that may be difficult to articulate verbally.
- **The power of "I".** When expressing your emotions to others, use "I" statements to convey your feelings clearly without blaming or attacking. For example, say, "I feel hurt when..." instead of "You always make me feel..."
- **Take a break.** If you find yourself overwhelmed by your emotions, step away from the situation, engage in a calming activity, and return to it when you feel more composed.

11. Trust Your Gut

Your intuition is a powerful tool that can help you make decisions and guide you through life's ups and downs. It's that little voice inside your head that tells you whether something feels right or wrong.

But why is intuition so important, especially for teenagers? Well, as you grow up and navigate the world, you'll face all kinds of challenging situations and decisions. From deciding what classes to take to figuring out how to deal with peer pressure, you'll encounter numerous situations where your intuition can be incredibly helpful.

That's because your intuition is often informed by your past experiences and knowledge. It's like your subconscious mind has a whole library of information that can help guide your decisions. For example, if you've had bad experiences with certain types of people in the past, your intuition might alert you to be wary of similar individuals in the future.

Of course, it isn't foolproof, and it's not something you should rely on exclusively. It's important to balance your intuition with rational thinking and careful decision-making. But when you learn to trust your gut and pay attention to your intuition, you'll find that it can be a valuable and empowering tool in navigating life's challenges.

Tips for Strengthening Your Intuition

The great thing about intuition is that you can work on improving it. It just takes a little bit of practice and intention, of course!

- **Start testing your hunches more often.** If you get a feeling about something that might happen, write those hunches down, and after a while, come back to see how often you were right. If you see your hunches coming true, that might give you more confidence to trust yourself more often.
- **Use your body as the compass.** If you get an uncomfortable feeling when you are attempting to make a decision, pay attention. Does it feel heavy? Sure, it could be a sign of stress and anxiety, but it could also be the sound of your intuition ringing loud and clear.
- **Have a break from your regular routine.** So, if you usually walk or run a specific route, take a break from it and try a different way. When we're used to "sameness," it can be all that more difficult to be sensitive to the voices of our intuition.
- **Always make sure that you're in alignment with your values.** Your mind will sometimes try to steer you away from integrity, but your intuition never will. Teach yourself to become more comfortable with how you feel when you are betraying your own trust—your own self. Start focusing on what it looks and feels like when you are in alignment with your values.

12. Take Care of Yourself

Our emotions affect how we treat ourselves and the world around us. I mean, ever notice how much more pleasant company we tend to be when we're happy and excited, in a bubble of bliss? And when we're cranky and worried, we're about as pleasant as a glass of sour milk? That is where self-care comes in.

Imagine self-care as giving yourself a hefty dose of goodness. It's like giving your soul, mind, body, and spirit a refreshing drink all at once. With busy schedules and never-ending tasks, it can be easy to forget to look after yourself.

You see, self-care is about more than just pampering yourself or indulging in occasional treats. It's about creating a sustainable lifestyle that promotes your overall health and happiness. When you prioritize self-care, you acknowledge that you matter, that your well-being is important, and that you deserve to be taken care of.

One of the key reasons self-care is vital is that it helps prevent burnout. As a teenager, you face a myriad of challenges: school pressures, extracurricular activities, social dynamics, and the uncertainty of the future. It's a lot to handle, and without proper self-care, it's easy to become overwhelmed and exhausted. By incorporating self-care practices into your daily routine, you give yourself the opportunity to recharge and replenish your energy.

Self-care is essential for maintaining good mental health. Adolescence is a time of immense growth and self-discovery, but it can also be a time of heightened stress, anxiety, and self-doubt. Engaging in activities that promote relaxation, such as practicing mindfulness or engaging in hobbies you enjoy, can help reduce stress levels and improve your overall well-being.

Self-care comes in different shapes and forms; it's not a one-size-fits-all approach, which is pretty spectacular if you think about it. We're all different, so on any given day, our self-care needs are going to differ as well. So, let's dive into some self-care tips you might want to try for yourself.

Physical Self-Care

- Make sure to get at least 7–8 hours of sleep every night to help your body recover and repair.
- Find physical activities that you enjoy and do them regularly. It could be anything from playing basketball to dancing to yoga.
- Incorporate nutrient-dense and nourishing food to your body, such as fruits, vegetables, whole grains, and lean protein.
- Make sure to maintain good oral hygiene, bathe regularly, and wear clean clothes to feel refreshed and put together.

Emotional Self-Care

- Writing down your thoughts and feelings can help you acknowledge your emotions and gain a better understanding of them.
- Engage in mindfulness practices like daily gratitude, meditation, deep breathing, or yoga to help you feel grounded and reduce stress.
- Seek support from friends, family members, counselors, or trusted adults. Sharing your emotions with someone can provide relief and help you feel less alone.

Social Self-Care

- Call or send a text message to a close friend.
- Suggest a milkshake and cake date with a friend or sibling.
- Participation in community service activities can help you feel good and create meaningful connections with others.
- If you're fortunate enough to have one, pets can also be a great source of comfort and support when you're feeling a little down. They're always there to listen and cuddle when you need it.

13. Manage Stress

"I can't take it anymore. I'm so stressed out," I huffed, slumping down in my chair and rubbing my temples. My mom looked sympathetically at me from across the table.

"I know it's tough, honey," she said. "But stress is a part of life. The key is learning how to manage it."

I rolled my eyes. "Great, another thing I have to learn how to do. Like I have time for that!"

But as the days went on, I realized that my mom had a point. I was constantly anxious about school and social stuff, and it was making me miserable. I needed to find a way to deal with all this stress.

That's when I started researching different techniques for managing stress. I learned that exercise was a great way to boost my mood and reduce anxiety. So, I started going for a quick jog around the park every morning before school. It wasn't always easy to drag myself out of bed, but I found that it made a big difference in how I felt throughout the day.

I also started practicing mindfulness, which is basically just focusing on the present moment and trying to quiet your thoughts. It felt weird at first, but I found that it helped me feel more in control when things got hectic. Of course, there were still plenty of times when I felt like I was at the end of my rope, but I started to realize that I had more control over my stress than I thought. By taking small steps, I gradually regained a sense of control over my life.

Okay, so let's talk about stress and what it really is. Simply put, it's just how our bodies respond to things when we feel overwhelmed. What happens is that the body releases these hormones called cortisol and adrenaline that give out something that's kind of like an energy boost, which is also known as the "fight or flight" response because it helps you react quickly in dangerous situations. But when we're stressed, the brain automatically thinks we're in danger all the time, even if we aren't. That's what makes it feel like we're always on edge.

So, what causes stress? Honestly, it can be a lot of things. Schoolwork, sports, social situations, family stuff—anything that feels like a lot to handle can be stressful. And what's stressful for one person might be totally fine for someone else. It's really subjective.

Stress isn't always necessarily a bad thing, either. Believe it or not, a little bit of it can actually be good for you. It can help you stay alert and focused and motivate you to work harder. The problem is when you're feeling stressed out all the time. That's when it can start affecting your health and your happiness.

Learning to Identify Your Stress Triggers

Learning what it is that triggers your stress is a great first step you can take toward learning what kinds of situations get you all worked up. That act alone increases your self-awareness and teaches you how to take care of your well-being. I know that it can sound a bit challenging, but with simple steps, it can be a lot easier for you.

- **Pay more attention to your body and its reactions.** Are there certain environments that make your tummy feel uneasy or like it is dropping? Being aware and mindful of these sensations that arise will give you small but valuable clues about the very things that are your biggest causes of stress.
- **Think about school or your extracurricular activities.** How do you feel when you have to approach a specific task, or when it's time to practice? Do you dread it? How do your teachers or coaches make you feel when they walk into the room?
- **Assess your personal life.** How are your relationships with your friends or siblings? Do interactions with them leave you feeling more drained and upset? I know it may seem that they are a usual part of your life, but that is also where stress can come from.

Tips on Managing Your Stress

- **Dance away the drama.** Turn up the volume and let your body groove! Dancing not only boosts your mood but also releases those tension knots in your muscles. So, put on your favorite tunes and dance like no one's watching. Bonus points for silly dance moves!
- **Create a Zen Den.** Find a cozy corner in your room and transform it into your personal Zen Den. Decorate it with fairy lights, comfy cushions, and calming scents. This sacred space will be your refuge when stress strikes. Take a few minutes each day to meditate, journal, or simply chill out in your Zen Den.
- **Unleash your inner Picasso.** Grab some paintbrushes, colored pencils, or even a simple pen and paper. Channel your stress into creativity and let your imagination run wild. Draw, paint, or doodle your heart out.
- **Laugh it off.** Laughter truly is the best medicine. Watch a hilarious sitcom, scroll through funny memes, or have a joke-off with your friends. Laughing releases tension and instantly lifts your spirits.
- **Power down for peace.** I know it's tempting to binge-watch your favorite shows or scroll endlessly through social media, but too much screen time can add to your stress. Turn off your devices for a designated period each day. Instead, engage in activities like reading, listening to music, or having meaningful conversations with loved ones.
- **Treat yourself to a self-care extravaganza.** Pamper yourself! Take a long bubble bath, indulge in your favorite face mask, or treat yourself to a decadent dessert. Self-care is essential for managing stress. So go ahead and spoil yourself. You deserve it!

14. It's Okay to Feel Sad Sometimes

I think sadness gets such a bad rap. It's often viewed as a negative emotion that we should try to avoid at all costs. But the truth is, sadness is natural and necessary, and can actually be beneficial.

For starters, it can be a great motivator. When we feel sad, we are often compelled to make changes in our lives to improve our situation. For example, if we're feeling sad about a friendship that isn't working out, we might be motivated to seek out friendships with others whose values and interests are more aligned to our own.

It also helps us appreciate the good things in life even more. When we experience sadness, it allows us to see the world in a completely different way than when things are going well. It can help us better understand and appreciate the happy moments when they come around.

15. Seek Support When You Need It

Life, much like climbing a mountain, is a thrilling yet challenging journey that demands strength, perseverance, and resilience. Just as every climber faces moments of fear and limitations, we, too encounter daunting challenges in our everyday lives. It's natural to want to conquer them independently, to show ourselves and those around us that we are strong and resilient. But the truth is, we all need help sometimes, especially when the situation we find ourselves in is out of our control.

Just as mountain climbers rely on their team, it's essential to build a support system of people around you who can offer guidance and assistance when you need it. It may be a friend who lends an ear to listen, a teacher who offers advice, or a therapist who provides professional support. Best of all, you can also be the person that someone turns to in their time of need.

Always remember that asking for help is not a sign of weakness but of strength. It takes courage to admit you need help and to reach out to others.

16. Don't Sweat the Small Stuff

In the rollercoaster of teenage years, it can be easy to get caught up in the whirlwind of emotions, drama, and daily challenges. However, one of the most valuable lessons you can learn is not to sweat the small stuff.

Why? Because life is a precious gift, and time is one of your most valuable assets. When you focus on every little problem, drama, or imperfection, you waste that precious resource. It's like zooming in too close on a painting and missing the breathtaking masterpiece.

So, if you're someone who gets easily bogged down by the small stuff, try taking a step back and noticing the beauty in the world around you. Whether it's a beautiful sunrise, a kind word from a friend, or a good cup of steaming hot cocoa in the morning, these little moments of joy and wonder can help you navigate life's stressors with grace and ease.

One, two, or even ten years from now, there are certain things that won't even matter. You'll look back and realize that stressing about them was all for nothing.

- **That bad hair day.** Remember that time when your hair just refused to cooperate? Well, guess what? A year from now, you won't even remember it. So, embrace the messy hair, rock a funky hat, or laugh it off. Life's too short to stress about a few rebellious strands.
- **Fashion faux pas.** We've all had those moments when we look back at old photos and cringe at our outfit choices. But here's the thing: Fashion trends change faster than you can say "wardrobe malfunction." So, wear what makes you happy, experiment with your style, and don't worry about being a fashion icon. Your confidence will always be your best accessory.

- **That embarrassing moment.** Remember that time you tripped in front of your crush? Embarrassing, right? But here's the silver lining: Embarrassing moments make the best stories later on! Trust me, a year from now, you'll be laughing about it with your friends. So, embrace the awkwardness and let it become a part of your unique journey.
- **The popularity contest.** In the grand scheme, popularity doesn't define your worth. The number of followers, likes, or comments won't matter a year from now—unless you have dreams of being a social media influencer. Focus on cultivating genuine connections with people who appreciate you for who you are. Quality over quantity, always!
- **That test you bombed.** We've all had those moments when we thought our world would crumble because of a bad grade. But here's the truth: One test does not define your intelligence or your future success. Learn from your mistakes, work hard, and remember that growth comes from perseverance, not perfection.
- **That petty drama.** Drama, drama, drama! It might feel like the end of the world when you're caught up in it, but trust me, a year from now, it won't even matter. Choose to surround yourself with positive vibes and let go of unnecessary conflicts. Life's too short to waste on petty drama.
- **The perfect social media feed.** Maintaining a picture-perfect social media feed can be exhausting. But here's the secret: The most memorable moments aren't always captured on camera. Embrace the imperfections, the silly faces, and the unfiltered moments. Real life is messy, and that's what makes it beautiful.

Remember, it's the bigger dreams and ambitions that deserve your attention, so don't let the small stuff hold you back from reaching your full potential.

17. Look After Your Mental Health

Mental health is not something to be taken lightly. Learning to identify the possible signs of declining mental health is important, both for yourself and those around you. Here are some signs you should look out for:

- Withdrawing from friends and family, or becoming unusually aggressive.
- Sudden or extreme mood swings.
- Changes in sleep patterns: That's either sleeping too much or too little.
- Changes in appetite that lead to either dramatic weight loss or gain.
- Difficulty concentrating. This may be a sign that you need to start prioritizing rest or alone time some more.
- You start losing interest in activities that you once enjoyed.
- Mental health concerns can also manifest as physical symptoms such as headaches, stomach aches, or fatigue.

If you recognize any of these signs, reach out for help.

Be Your Own Cheerleader

Nurturing Self-Esteem and Positivity

We don't celebrate ourselves enough. So many of us are waiting for others to give us praise or a well-done sticker to confirm our worth. But do you know what I think works and feels much better? When that support comes from within—when it comes from *you*.

When you only seek approval from others, you can become anxious and unsure of yourself. But when you take the time to recognize your achievements and growth, you build your confidence and self-esteem.

So go ahead, give yourself a pat on the back, and keep striving for success!

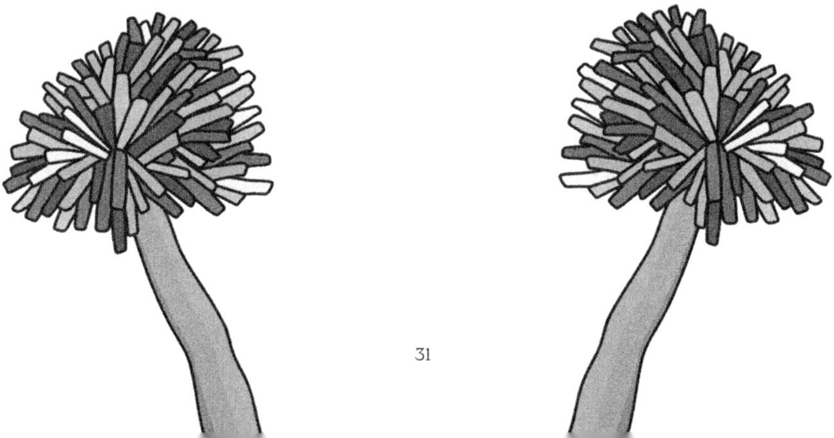

18. Pursue Progress, Not Perfection

So many of us want to have things all figured out; we want to control the outcome of every situation and encounter that we have. I guess that's understandable.

It's natural to strive for excellence and do our best, but here's the thing—perfectionism is overrated. Yup, you heard me right! So, let's dive into why aiming for perfection might not be as ideal as it seems.

First off, perfectionism can put too much pressure on you. When you set impossibly high standards for yourself, you can end up stressing out and feeling overwhelmed. You may become afraid of making mistakes because you think they define your worth. But guess what? Making mistakes is part of being human. It's through mistakes that we learn, grow, and develop resilience. So, instead of fearing mistakes, embrace them as valuable opportunities for growth.

Perfectionism also often leads to procrastination. When fixated on achieving flawless results, you may delay starting a task altogether because you're afraid of falling short. This can lead to missed opportunities and added stress as deadlines approach. Remember, it's better to start imperfectly and make progress than to wait for the "perfect" moment that may never come.

When you constantly worry about meeting impossibly high standards, you may become afraid of taking risks and exploring new ideas. But, creativity thrives on experimentation, exploration, and even failure. By embracing imperfection, you can open yourself up to new possibilities and discover unique solutions to problems.

So, stop striving for perfection and instead focus on progress. Trust me, you'll still get to where you need to, with a whole lot less stress and drama.

19. Practice Positive Thinking

So what is positive thinking? It's basically a way of looking at things that helps you stay positive even when things get tough. When you have a positive mindset, you can turn problems into opportunities to learn and grow. It helps you feel hopeful and optimistic, even when things seem really hard. This kind of thinking can give you the power to take control of your life and confidently bounce back from setbacks. Plus, it's great for your mental health and can even help you build better relationships with others.

While positive thinking can be transformative, it is essential to acknowledge that life encompasses both highs and lows. Toxic positivity begins when we suppress genuine emotions such as sadness, anger, or frustration, believing that only positive emotions should prevail. True positive thinking does not deny or invalidate negative emotions but instead encourages a healthy way of processing them. It is crucial to embrace authenticity and recognize that it is normal to experience a range of emotions. By allowing yourself to feel and express these emotions, you create space for healing, growth, and genuine positivity.

The power of positive thinking also lies in its ability to inspire and empower you, changing your life and the lives of those around you. By embracing positive thinking while avoiding the pitfalls of toxic positivity, you can create a mindset that allows you to face challenges with resilience, authenticity, and compassion.

You might be reading this and thinking: That sounds all well and good, but how and where do I even begin cultivating a positive mindset? Well, I have just the tips and pointers to guide you in the right direction.

Challenge Your Negative Thoughts and Beliefs

As much as we may want to avoid them, our negative thoughts have a way of sneaking into our minds, like uninvited guests, ready to lead us astray from our goals and aspirations. They whisper in our ears, telling us that we're not good enough, that we'll never succeed, and that our efforts are futile. Their persistence can make it incredibly difficult to operate on a day-to-day basis, draining our energy and clouding our judgment.

Just imagine waking up in the morning with a sense of dread, knowing that the negative thoughts are waiting eagerly to invade your mind. It becomes a challenge to muster the motivation to get out of bed to face the world with confidence and optimism. The weight of these thoughts can feel suffocating, like an anchor that keeps us stuck in a sea of negativity.

But here's the thing: You have the power to break free from this cycle. You can reframe your thoughts to challenge the negative beliefs that hold you back. It takes courage and resilience, but with practice, you can learn to recognize these negative thoughts for what they are: illusions that have no basis in reality.

One strategy is to replace negative thoughts with positive affirmations. Instead of allowing self-doubt to consume you, you can consciously choose to focus on your strengths and achievements. By shifting your perspective and acknowledging your worth, you can begin to silence the negative chatter in your mind. On the following page are some affirmations that you can use to anchor yourself when it seems the thoughts are taking over.

Another powerful tool you can use to challenge negative thoughts is mindfulness. When you practice mindfulness, you observe your thoughts without judgment, allowing them to come and go without getting entangled in their negativity. This practice helps you cultivate a greater sense of self-awareness and empowers you to make conscious choices about how you want to respond to your thoughts.

Positive affirmations

- I am worthy of love and respect just as I am.
- I have the power to overcome any challenge that comes my way.
- I am capable of achieving my goals and dreams.
- I am surrounded by supportive and uplifting people.
- I embrace change and see it as an opportunity for growth.
- I am in control of my own happiness and choose to focus on the positive.
- I am grateful for all the blessings in my life.
- I trust in my abilities and have confidence in myself.
- I choose to release all negative thoughts and replace them with positive ones.
- I am deserving of success and abundance in all areas of my life.
- I am resilient and can bounce back from setbacks.
- I am loved, appreciated, and valued by those around me.
- I am confident in expressing my true self and embracing my uniqueness.
- I deserve to prioritize my well-being so I won't let negative thoughts or things I can't control take over.

20. Say Goodbye to Limiting Self-Beliefs

Have you ever felt like you were being held prisoner by your own thoughts? Maybe you've thought, "I'm not smart enough," or "I'll never be good at that." Well, my friend, those are called limiting self-beliefs, and they can have a big impact on how you see yourself and what you believe you can achieve.

So, what exactly are limiting self-beliefs? They're those negative thoughts or beliefs you may have about yourself that hold you back from realizing your true potential. They can make you doubt your abilities, feel unworthy, or even prevent you from taking risks and trying new things. These beliefs can be like invisible walls that confine you within your comfort zone, preventing you from reaching for the stars.

Now, you might be wondering how these limiting self-beliefs even start. Well, they can come from a variety of sources. Sometimes, it's the result of comparing yourself to others. You may see someone else succeed and think, "I could never do that." But here's the thing—comparing yourself to others is a recipe for disaster. You're a unique individual with different strengths and abilities. What someone else achieves doesn't diminish your potential. You have your own unique path to walk.

Another common source of limiting self-beliefs is the influence of others. Sometimes, people unintentionally project their own fears and insecurities onto you. They might discourage you from pursuing your dreams or tell you you're not good enough. But remember, their opinions don't define you. You have the power to choose what you believe about yourself.

Or maybe you've faced failure or rejection in the past, and now you're afraid to try again. But here's a secret: Failure is not a reflection of your worth or potential. It's proof that you're trying, so embrace failures as learning opportunities and keep moving forward.

The good thing you can hold onto when it comes to negative beliefs or thoughts is that you can reprogram your brain to silence your inner critic. This is what you can do:

- **Become aware of self-limiting beliefs.** The first step to change will always be awareness. You first have to start by recognizing those damaging thoughts that continue to play on in your head. Watch out for sentences that begin with words like, "I can't..." "I'm no good at..." and "I'll never be able to..." Try adding the word "yet" to these sentences and see what a difference it makes.
- **Challenge the validity of your self-limiting thoughts.** Is there any actual evidence that those thoughts are true, or is it just your brain trying to talk you out of doing something? Most of the time, you'll find that it is the latter. So ask yourself, "Why am I thinking these thoughts?" "Where are they coming from?" and "Is this even true?"
- **Make a conscious choice to stop believing those beliefs.** You get to decide that you will no longer believe in the lies that these thoughts are feeding you. Give yourself permission to let go of those things—you're more than allowed to do so.
- **Try to uncover where the belief originated.** Is there a particular instance that made you feel a certain way or believe a certain thing? By acknowledging where the beliefs come from, you reduce and diminish their power over you.
- **Become intentional about building new and healthier beliefs.** Now, this part requires work. When those incessant thoughts pop up, you have to catch yourself and stop them. When you call yourself out for believing too deeply in a negative thought or notion, or break down an old belief and build a new one, you are rewiring your brain. So don't stop when it's hard. Progress happens when we show up each day in small ways.

21. Like Yourself

It doesn't matter much what other people think of you. What matters most is what you think of yourself. Do you like yourself? Do you have your own back? Are you willing to put yourself first? Those are the things you should be asking yourself.

In a world teeming with opinions and judgments, it can be easy to succumb to the pressure of seeking validation from others. However, the truth remains that what others think of you should hold little weight compared to what you think of yourself. The key lies in developing a strong sense of self-worth and embracing self-acceptance.

When you ask yourself, "Do I like myself?" it goes beyond a superficial assessment. It delves into the core of your being and forces you to confront your true feelings about who you are. Self-liking is not about arrogance or conceit; it is about recognizing your strengths, acknowledging your flaws, and accepting yourself as a whole. Having your own back means being your own advocate, standing up for yourself, and treating yourself with kindness and compassion. It involves acknowledging your worthiness and not allowing external factors to define your value. By having your own back, you become your own ally, ready to defend your beliefs, dreams, and boundaries.

When you prioritize what you think of yourself over the opinions of others, you cultivate a strong and resilient mindset. Your self-perception becomes the foundation upon which you build your confidence and self-esteem. It enables you to navigate life's challenges with greater ease and authenticity.

So, how do you cultivate a better self-image? I'll tell you.

Be Your Own Number-One Fan

This one is giving #maincharachterenergy. Imagine yourself as the star of your own show. Just like the roaring crowd in a packed stadium, let your self-love and confidence take center stage. You are the lead character in your life's story, and it's crucial to root for yourself wholeheartedly. Remember, it's not about winning a popularity contest; it's about valuing yourself, appreciating your unique quirks, and celebrating your individuality. The applause starts from within.

Embrace Your True Reflection

Picture your self-image as a canvas awaiting your artistic touch. You have the power to paint it with vibrant colors that reflect your genuine essence. Don't get caught up in comparing your intricately designed self-portrait to someone else's; each stroke is uniquely yours. Instead, focus on the qualities that make you special—your sense of humor, your passions, or your never-give-up attitude. Your true reflection is a masterpiece waiting to be appreciated.

Fill Your Self-Love Cup

Imagine self-love as a cup that needs to be filled regularly. It's easy to get caught up in the day-to-day, but remember, you still need to take a break. Think of nurturing your self-image as a way to refuel, like taking a deep breath when you're running on empty. Discover activities that uplift your spirits, whether it's going for a walk in nature, dancing to your favorite tunes, or journaling your thoughts. Remember, by taking care of yourself, you will be able to live life in a way that feels—and is—inspiring!

I want to remind you that you're not always going to like yourself every single day of every week, and that's okay. There will be days where you wish the whole world would just leave you alone, but on those days, you have to remember you are worthy of love, acceptance, and respect.

22. Be Grateful

There's something about gratitude... something about it that lifts the veil before our eyes and makes us see the world in a completely new light. My grandmother used to say that to see with the eyes of gratitude is to see with the heart.

As you grow and mature, you begin to appreciate the little things more. The vibrant colors of the sunset, the sound of laughter from those you care about, and the comfort of being at home become even more special. It's amazing how life's simple pleasures can bring so much joy and wonder.

Gratitude teaches us to slow down and savor the present moment. It encourages us to pause and reflect on the goodness that exists within and around us. In a world that often moves at a dizzying pace, gratitude serves as an anchor, grounding us in the here and now. It reminds us to be fully present, to embrace the richness of each passing moment, and to find joy in the simplest of pleasures.

But gratitude is not just about acknowledging the good times; it also teaches us resilience during challenging moments. When faced with adversity, gratitude helps us find silver linings and lessons within the hardships. It reminds us that even in the darkest of times, there is always something to be grateful for—be it the support of a friend, the strength we discover within ourselves, or the opportunity for growth.

Practicing gratitude is a skill that can be honed through conscious effort. It starts with cultivating a mindset of appreciation and actively seeking out the good things in our lives. Whether through journaling, meditation, or simply taking a few moments each day to reflect, we can train ourselves to shift our focus from what is lacking to what is abundant.

Here are some small ways you can be grateful each day:

- **Acknowledge the good things that happen to you.** This can be a super fun activity to do if you think about it. You can do it with your family when sitting around the dinner table. And remember those moments of gratitude, don't have to be big for them to matter.
- **Use a gratitude journal as a reminder.** This one is a lot like the first one, but instead of saying and mentioning the things out loud, you're writing them down. You can write things down like the fact that you woke up today, or if it was a particularly difficult day, you can mention the fact that you made it through the day! I don't know about you, but I definitely think that's something to be glad about.
- **Say thanks to your friends/siblings/family/to people in general.** I don't think we realize this but saying thanks to people can make the world of a difference. Letting people know that they matter reinforces the message that they have a special place in this world and are appreciated.

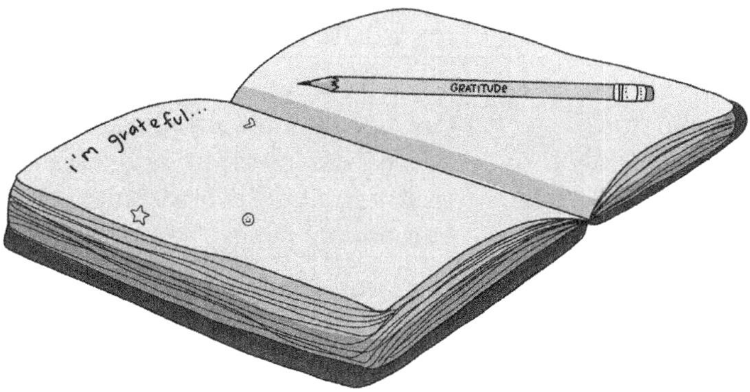

23. Reframe Negative Thinking

Reframing thoughts is an incredibly empowering practice and can significantly improve your mental health and overall well-being. Simply put, reframing is about changing how you look at a situation or experience.

Picture yourself wearing a pair of glasses with lenses that add a distinct tint to everything you look at. You see the whole world through these tinted lenses. In the same way, our thoughts can also be tinted or biased, which can affect how you experience situations and events.

Reframing helps you change these tinted lenses, change how you see things, and shift your thoughts in a more positive direction. It is a powerful and effective tool because thoughts profoundly impact our emotions, actions, and overall mood.

Here are a few ways in which you can practice reframing situations when negative thoughts pop in:

Instead of saying this to yourself	Say this
I am such a failure because I didn't make it on the A-team.	Rejection is a normal part of life, and it doesn't and shouldn't get to define my worth.
I don't think I can handle this situation, it's way too overwhelming for me.	This situation is challenging, yes, but I know that I have faced overwhelming circumstances in the past. I can take one step at a time and handle it.
I am always so awkward in social situations.	I do get nervous sometimes, but I am more than capable of building meaningful relationships with people.

24. Laugh at Yourself

Life can be tough, and a hot mess as well. But it's important to not take it too seriously. One of the best things you can do for yourself is to learn to laugh at yourself. It's a great way to let yourself loosen a little.

When you can laugh at yourself, you're showing you're not afraid to make mistakes. It takes a lot of courage to put yourself out there and take risks. But when you can laugh at your own mistakes, it helps you bounce back faster and shows that you're resilient. Plus, laughing at yourself is just plain fun! There's nothing better than being able to laugh off a silly mistake or a moment of embarrassing clumsiness. It brings joy to your day, and it's contagious. When you can make others laugh, too, you're spreading that joy around.

Here are a few ways to get started on laughing at yourself a little more:

- **Find the humor.** When things go wrong, try to find the humor in it. Instead of getting upset or frustrated, look for the silver lining. What's the funny part of the situation?
- **Be playful.** Life doesn't always have to be so serious. Take a playful approach to life, and it'll be easier to laugh at yourself. Be silly, joke around, and don't be afraid to be a little bit weird.
- **Share your stories.** When you're able to laugh at yourself, it's a lot easier to share your embarrassing stories with others, which helps create deeper connections, too.

Oh, and don't forget—laughing at yourself doesn't mean you're not taking life seriously. It simply means you can find joy and humor in the ups and downs.

So, the next time you make a mistake or do something silly, try to laugh it off. You'll feel better for it, and those around you will appreciate your lightheartedness.

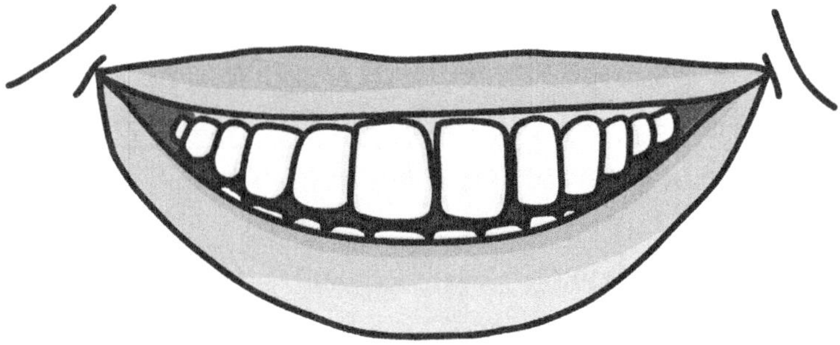

25. Smile More

When I say smile more, I'm not saying do it because it makes you that much prettier, but because it makes the world around you all that much more beautiful as well. A smile, so simple yet so powerful, has the extraordinary ability to transform not only your own life but the lives of those around you.

Imagine a world where everyone embraced the magic of a smile. Picture the streets bustling with people whose faces light up with genuine joy as they exchange smiles with one another. In this world, people open up to strangers, share kind words, and offer a sense of belonging simply through the power of their heartfelt smiles.

When you smile, you invite happiness into your life. You create a ripple effect, brightening the days of those you encounter and uplifting their spirits.

So, go on, show your best set of pearly whites, and share your smile with the world.

26. Have Fun!

I used to be one of those people who waited for that assignment to be handed in or that note to be ticked off my to-do list before actually enjoying myself. But as time went on, a single question kept recurring: Why can't I allow myself to be here, present, regardless of what I have and haven't done yet?

Reflecting on my journey, I realize the key to genuinely having fun lies in embracing the present moment, irrespective of the tasks and responsibilities that lie ahead. It's a mindset shift that every smart girl should adopt. Here's what I've learned along the way:

- **Embrace the power of now.** The present moment is all we truly have. Instead of constantly dwelling on what needs to be done in the future, remind yourself to be fully present in the here and now. Take a deep breath, observe your surroundings, and engage with the present moment.
- **Embrace spontaneity.** Smart girls tend to be planners, meticulously organizing every aspect of their lives. While planning is important, don't be afraid to embrace spontaneity and go with the flow once in a while. Allow yourself to be open to new experiences and opportunities that may arise unexpectedly. Some of the best memories are often created in the spur of the moment.
- **Find joy in the simple things.** Happiness doesn't always come from grand gestures or extravagant events. Learn to appreciate the little things in life and find joy in the simple pleasures. It could be savoring a delicious smoothie, walking your dog in the park, or spending quality time with loved ones.
- **Have a whole load of fun.** Taking time for yourself and engaging in activities that bring you happiness will ultimately make you more productive, creative, and fulfilled in all areas of your life

You have the power to unlock the true joy and fulfillment that life has to offer. So go ahead, smart girl, and allow yourself to have fun—you've earned it!

Girl Talk

Building Authentic Connections

I had this English teacher back in high school, Mrs. Morgan. She was a petite woman with spectacles perched perpetually on the bridge of her nose, always seen with a book in her hand. She was stern but fair, and she had an uncanny knack for bringing stories to life in a way that made every student sit on the edge of their seat. However, it wasn't until the summer I left for college that I truly understood the depth of her wisdom and kindness.

Just days before I was set to embark on my college journey, I bumped into Mrs. Morgan at our small town's local bookstore. She was engrossed in a book, but when she saw me, her face lit up with a warm smile. "Ah! The future college student," she exclaimed, marking her place in the book with a finger. We exchanged pleasantries, and then she asked me how I was feeling about leaving for college. I hesitated, then confessed my fears and anxieties—the fear of the unknown, the pressure to succeed, the worry of making new friends. Mrs. Morgan listened quietly, nodding her head occasionally. When I finished, she gave me a thoughtful look and then reached for a nearby book. It was a copy of Harper Lee's *To Kill a Mockingbird*, a book we had dissected in her class.

She flipped to a dog-eared page and read aloud: "You never really understand a person until you consider things from his point of view... Until you climb inside of his skin and walk around in it." She closed the book and looked at me, her eyes twinkling behind her glasses. "Building authentic connections," she said, "is all about understanding, empathy, and genuine curiosity about others. It's about climbing into their skin and seeing the world from their perspective."

That conversation was, in a word, life-changing. It wasn't the last time I'd talk to Mrs. Morgan, but it was the moment that our teacher-student relationship evolved into a bond of genuine understanding and mutual respect. As I navigated through my college years and beyond, her advice about building authentic connections became my guiding principle, influencing my relationships, my career, and my life.

Every time I meet someone new, I think of that profound summer conversation with Mrs. Morgan in the bookstore. I remind myself to seek understanding, show empathy, and be genuinely curious. It's not always easy, but it's always rewarding. Because, as I learned from my old English teacher, authentic connections aren't just about shared interests or mutual benefits; they're about shared understanding and mutual respect. And that, I believe, is what truly makes life rich and meaningful.

In a society that encourages superficiality and masks, choosing authenticity in our communication is a revolutionary act. It requires courage to strip away the layers of pretense and reveal our true selves, to express our thoughts and emotions honestly and fearlessly. But in doing so, we create fertile ground for deep connections to flourish and meaningful relationships to take root.

27. Be an Active Listener

Most of us are pretty good at hearing what people say, but understanding them? That's a whole different story.

We often find ourselves nodding along, pretending to listen, while our minds wander and drift elsewhere. But understanding someone, connecting with their thoughts and emotions, requires a whole different level of attention and intention. This is where the art of actively listening comes into play.

Tips for becoming an active listener

- Look the speaker directly in the eyes when they are speaking. Eye contact is such an important part of face-to-face communication. It tells the speaker, "Hey, I'm actually listening to what you have to say," which is reassuring. But you also want to remember not to make too much eye contact because that can come across as a little creepy. So, try to find the balance between looking at the person and at the space around them.
- Pay attention to what the other person is saying with their body (the non-verbal communication cues they are sending out) or their facial expressions. Their tone of voice and how they hold their bodies can communicate how comfortable or uncomfortable a person actually feels around you.
- Don't interrupt. Let the person you're talking to speak and finish whatever it is they are saying. If you are constantly interrupting or not listening fully to what they say, you might give the impression that you think you're better than them, which is certainly not what you want to convey if you're trying to build a healthy relationship.
- Don't obsess too much about what you're going to say next—you can't listen and prepare at the same time.
- Ask questions. Questions show that you're interested in what the person is saying, and they're also a great way to clarify anything you might not be clear on.

28. Speak Loudly Without Words

The body speaks and says more than we sometimes want it to. You may be slouching and thinking to yourself, *Oh, this is just me in a relaxed state*, but someone else may think, *Oh, she looks a little dejected.* You may be wearing a frown on your face and thinking, *This is just my normal day-to-day, default facial expression*, but someone else may think, *Oh, that person is unapproachable.*

Body language is a powerful form of nonverbal communication that can make a lasting impression on those around you, whether you're aware of it or not. Understanding and utilizing body language can be valuable in building confidence, fostering positive relationships, and thriving in various social settings. So, let's explore some tips and tricks to help you make the most out of it.

First and foremost, let's start with the basics: posture. The way you carry yourself speaks volumes about your self-esteem and how you perceive the world. Stand or sit tall with your shoulders back and head held high and maintain an open posture. Avoid crossing your arms or hunching over, as this can make you appear closed off or disinterested. By maintaining a confident and open posture, you'll exude an air of self-assurance and approachability.

Gestures and facial expressions also play a significant role in conveying your thoughts and emotions. Avoid fidgeting or excessive hand movements, as they can be distracting and give the impression of nervousness or uncertainty. Instead, use purposeful and controlled gestures to emphasize your points or to show enthusiasm. A warm and genuine smile can work wonders in creating a positive and approachable vibe, making it easier for others to connect with you.

It's essential to be aware of your overall body language in different social situations. Tailoring your body language to suit the context can help you establish rapport and communicate effectively.

For instance, in a classroom setting, maintaining a more formal and composed demeanor can convey competence and diligence. On the other hand, at a party, you can relax a bit and let your body language reflect a more laid-back and friendly attitude.

Lastly, remember that body language is a two-way street. Paying attention to the body language of others can provide valuable insights into their thoughts and feelings, allowing you to respond appropriately. Look for signs of interest, such as leaning in, nodding, or maintaining eye contact, as they indicate engagement.

29. Be Assertive

Be assertive. I'm sure that's a phrase you've heard before, but what does it actually mean? Assertiveness is more than just a buzzword; it's a valuable skill that can empower you to express your thoughts, feelings, and needs in a clear and respectful manner.

Contrary to popular belief, being assertive does not mean being aggressive or confrontational. It's about finding a balance between passivity and aggression, where you can confidently communicate your desires while respecting the boundaries and opinions of others. It's about standing up for yourself, expressing your thoughts and emotions honestly, and advocating for your needs without undermining or disrespecting others. It's about taking up as much space as you want and need while granting people the same privilege to do so in their own right.

One of the key elements of assertiveness is effective communication. It involves expressing your thoughts and feelings directly and clearly, using "I" statements to express your perspective without blaming or attacking others. For example, instead of saying, "You always interrupt me and never listen," you can say, "I feel frustrated when I'm interrupted because it makes me feel like my thoughts and ideas aren't valued." By using "I" statements, you take ownership of your emotions and experiences, fostering open and honest communication.

Setting boundaries is another crucial aspect of assertiveness. It involves defining what is acceptable and unacceptable to you and communicating those boundaries to others. This can be particularly challenging as a teen girl, as societal expectations and pressures often make asserting your needs and preferences difficult. However, establishing healthy boundaries is essential for maintaining emotional well-being and self-respect. Practice saying "no" when necessary without feeling guilty or obligated to please others. Remember, your needs and boundaries are as valid as anyone else's. (I am not delving too deeply into the concept of boundary-setting here because we'll be discussing it later in the book.)

Building assertiveness skills takes practice and self-awareness. Start by identifying situations where you tend to be passive or aggressive and reflect on how you can respond assertively instead. Role-playing with a trusted friend or family member can also help you practice assertive communication in a safe environment. Additionally, cultivating self-confidence and self-esteem is vital for assertiveness. Recognize your own worth and value, and believe in your right to be heard and respected.

Being assertive may be challenging, and you might encounter resistance or pushback from others accustomed to your previous communication style. But it's important to stay true to yourself and persevere. As you assert yourself respectfully and confidently, you will gain the respect of those around you and create a positive change in your relationships and interactions.

Be fierce, and be unapologetic about that!

30. Advocate for Yourself

Self-advocacy is all about standing up for yourself. It's speaking up when you disagree with others and voicing your opinions—even when you feel most vulnerable. It's choosing not to attach your dignity to hurtful comments. It refusing to get involved in the kinds of arguments that aim to make you feel small. Oh, and it can also look like walking away, like disengaging from harmful conversations.

Self-advocacy is empowerment. It's about knowing your worth, understanding your rights, and never letting anyone diminish your value. It's learning to say "no" when needed and "yes" when it's right. It's about having the courage to make choices that align with your beliefs and values, even when those choices aren't popular or easy.

Just as a diamond has four main components—carat, cut, clarity, and color—self-advocacy, too, has four integral parts that make it shine bright:

- **Knowledge.** First and foremost, self-advocacy is about self-awareness. It's about knowing yourself—your strengths, likes, dislikes, dreams, and fears. It's about understanding your rights and responsibilities and being informed about the situations you find yourself in. Knowledge is power; the more you know about yourself, the better you can advocate for your needs and wants.
- **Assertiveness.** This is the strength behind self-advocacy. It's the courage to stand up for yourself, hold your ground when challenged, and persist when facing obstacles. It's about not letting fear or intimidation keep you silent. But remember, assertiveness isn't about being aggressive or confrontational; it's about being firm, fair, and respectful.

- **Decision-making.** Ultimately, self-advocacy is about making choices. It's about taking the knowledge you have, the communication skills you've developed, and the assertiveness you've cultivated and using them to make decisions that reflect your values and advance your goals.
- **Persistence.** This is about staying committed and determined to achieve your goals, even when few people believe in you or when you encounter challenges along the way. When you persist and push through, it is equivalent to saying, "I believe in myself, and I won't stop until I reach whatever it is that I am working towards."

You possess an unstoppable force within you. It's not about being defiant for defiance's sake but about embracing your worth, values, and voice. As you continue on your journey, never forget that self-advocacy is an act of radical self-love.

31. Master the Art of Small Talk

Making small talk used to terrify me. I dreaded getting stuck in awkward conversations at parties or with classmates. My heart would race, my mind would go blank, and I just wanted to escape any chitchat as quickly as possible. But I realized avoiding small talk was limiting my ability to connect with others. So I pushed myself to practice this essential skill. Let me tell you about the first time I really tried engaging in easy, breezy small talk.

I was in line at the cafeteria behind a girl from my math class. Normally I would avoid eye contact and not say anything. But I took a deep breath and said, "Hey! How's your day going so far?" I made a simple observation about the long lunch line to keep the conversation flowing.

We chatted about classes and favorite cafeteria foods. I asked questions and shared a funny story about the time I spilled my lunch tray. Sure, there were some awkward silences, but I just smiled and kept things moving.

After a few minutes, I thanked her for the nice chat and went on my way. It was such a rush realizing I had successfully made casual small talk and formed a mini-bond.

Being able to make small talk can be awkward at first, but trust me when I say that it's a skill that will come in handy in your teenage years and later on in life.

So here are some tips to help you master the art of small talk:

- Start by closely observing your surroundings before entering a conversation. Identify something in the environment that could naturally lead to an opening remark. Comment on the weather, a class you share, the school basketball team's win on the weekend—whatever is relevant. This gets the ball rolling.
- Most people like talking about themselves, so ask friendly questions to learn more about the other person while avoiding anything too personal early on. Ask open-ended questions.

These are questions that require more than a yes/no or one-word answer. For example: What are your hobbies? What is your favorite subject in school and why? Where is the most interesting place you've traveled to? These types of questions invite the other person to provide details, share stories and opinions that keep the conversation flowing.

- Listen closely to their responses so you can ask thoughtful follow-up questions and find common ground.
- Share a relevant opinion, experience, or fun fact about yourself to keep the exchange balanced and two-sided. But don't overshare or dominate the conversation. Your goal is to keep it light and mutually engaging.
- Don't stress too much about lulls in the conversation—they're perfectly natural. With more practice over time, small talk will become second nature. You'll recognize cues to smoothly continue or wrap up the chat.
- End on a positive note by smiling, thanking the other person for the conversation, and wishing them well.

Making small talk is a simple yet powerful way to form connections, meet new people, and brighten someone's day. So don't be afraid to start small talking. Like most things, it gets easier the more you do it.

That's it for another chapter. How are you feeling? Inspired? I sure hope so because that's the whole purpose of this book. To light up that fire. That spark. All of that life within you. And there's still more to come. In the next chapter, we navigate relationships and friendships to ensure they're as drama-free as possible.

Love, Respect, and Drama-Free

Nurturing Healthy Friendships and Relationships

I come from a family of storytellers. During Thanksgiving time, around a crackling fire, we'll open up and share stories about life, love, mishaps, and the best of all friendships. I've heard countless stories go around the fire, but the one that has stuck with me for as long as I can remember is one that my great aunt Catherine told us about a friend named Margaret.

Margaret and my great aunt grew up in the same small town and had been best friends since they were young. They did everything together, from playing dress-up to exploring the woods behind their houses. But as they got older and entered high school, their friendship started to unravel.

One day, Margaret started a rumor about my great aunt that was completely untrue. The rumor quickly spread around the school, and soon, my great aunt found herself the subject of malicious gossip and cruel taunts. She was devastated and didn't know what to do.

After the initial shock of the situation wore off, my great aunt decided that she needed to confront Margaret and find out why she had done such a hurtful thing. She invited her over to her house and asked her point-blank.

At first, Margaret was defensive and refused to admit to anything. But eventually, she broke down in tears and confessed that she had been jealous of my great aunt's popularity and had done what she did to try and bring her down.

It wasn't an easy conversation, but it was a necessary one. After that day, Margaret and my great aunt worked to rebuild their friendship on a foundation of trust and respect. They were never as close as they once were, but they were able to maintain a cordial and drama-free relationship.

So, what can we learn from this story? First and foremost, it's important to always be honest and respectful with our friends. If we're feeling jealous or angry, it's better to talk it out rather than taking it out on someone else. And if we find ourselves on the receiving end of hurtful behavior, it's important to speak up for ourselves and confront the situation head-on.

Of course, this is easier said than done. It can be really scary to have those tough conversations and put ourselves out there. But the rewards of building strong, drama-free friendships are well worth it. When we have a solid support system of kind, respectful friends, we're better equipped to handle the ups and downs of life with grace and humor.

So, as you navigate your own relationships with your peers, remember the story of Margaret and my great aunt. Choose your words and actions wisely, and don't be afraid to hold yourself and your friends accountable for respectful behavior. And most of all, take the time to nurture those special bonds that make life worth living.

32. Be a Good Friend

Now, let's address an age old question. Is being a good friend all about having identical interests? Well, while it's definitely fun to geek out over the same stuff, like binge-watching your favorite series or discussing the latest viral memes, it's not the be-all and end-all of friendship. True friendship is about embracing our differences and celebrating the unique quirks that make us who we are. It's like having a cool mixtape with diverse tracks that somehow harmonize perfectly.

Oh, and speaking of harmony, let's talk about common dislikes and enemies. Sure, it can be amusing to bond over a mutual annoyance or vent about that horrendous math teacher who loves giving pop quizzes. But let's not build friendships on negativity alone. A solid friendship is built on a foundation of positivity and support, where you uplift and encourage each other. So, ditch the enemy list and focus on spreading good vibes instead.

When it comes to being a good friend, consistency is key. Imagine having a friend who mysteriously appears and disappears like a ninja in the night. It can be frustrating, right? Whether it's a weekly hangout, a quick text check-in, or a virtual game night, make an effort to be present consistently in each other's lives. Reliability ensures your friendship thrives through thick and thin.

Being a good friend is a marvelous blend of shared interests, positive vibes, attentive listening, and consistent presence. It's being someone who's always ready to laugh, lend a hand, encourage, or provide a shoulder to lean on. It's about building an unbreakable bond and sprinkling a bit of wit and humor along the way. It doesn't have to be rocket science, but it does take effort, empathy, and a dash of fun.

33. Choose Kindness

Kindness is a universal language; one that is understood by everyone and will never go out of style. When you choose kindness, you are actively contributing to the creation of a better world, not just for yourself but for everyone around you, too.

One of the ways you can make kindness an everyday part of your life is by choosing to not engage in gossip. I know how tempting (and fun) it can be to moan about people behind their backs. But you know what smart girls do? They address and try to resolve conflict, even when it's hard for them. It takes a lot of courage to confront conflict head-on rather than letting it fester and potentially escalate into something more damaging.

Choosing kindness, believe it or not, is also about choosing the higher ground. When you take the higher ground, you're not just being nice or pretentious. It's a way of being empathetic and showing understanding and respect to others, which can have a great positive ripple effect. It's also about being inclusive and not being dismissive when people share their ideas and opinions with you. It is about making your presence a place where your friends, peers, and acquaintances can be themselves without shame.

So, where you can, offer a kind smile, a listening ear, or a hug to someone who seems like they need it. Be that ray of sunshine, that glimmer of light on the days when it seems like there is little to no light at all.

34. Build Bridges, Not Barriers

Resolving conflict is about as comfortable as trying to ignore one of those embarrassing moments that happened to you a while ago. But trust me, it's worth it!

Why is it so important, you ask? Well, let me break it down for you. First off, it saves you from unnecessary drama. Who needs that extra stress in their life? By calmly addressing the issue at hand, you can avoid turning a tiny disagreement into a full-blown soap opera. Also, it helps maintain healthy relationships. Think about it: Constantly arguing and holding grudges can strain even the strongest bonds. By finding a practical solution, you can keep the peace and ensure your friendships stay intact. Plus, your friends will appreciate your level-headedness and maturity.

It's also a valuable life skill that you're going to use when you're much older. By learning to communicate effectively, compromise, and find common ground, you're setting yourself up for success in future relationships, both personal and professional.

Now, I won't lie to you. Resolving conflict proactively isn't always a walk in the park. It takes effort, patience, and a sprinkle of humility. So let's talk about how to do it.

One of the keys to resolving conflicts is effective communication. It's important to approach the situation with an open mind and a willingness to listen to the other person's perspective. When you disagree with someone, it can be easy to get caught up in your emotions and lose sight of the bigger picture. That's why it's crucial to remain calm and focused and avoid making assumptions or jumping to conclusions.

Another important aspect of conflict resolution is finding a middle ground or compromise that works for everyone involved. This requires flexibility, creativity, and a willingness to seek mutually beneficial solutions. It's also important to take responsibility for your actions and to own up to any mistakes or misunderstandings that may have contributed to the conflict.

Now I've given you the theoretical knowledge needed to help you navigate conflict, let's look at some practical scenarios that show how you can express your opinions respectfully and assertively.

Scenario: You're working on a group project, and one of your group members keeps interrupting you when you're speaking.
Example: "Hey, I appreciate your enthusiasm, but I'd like to finish my thought before you jump in. It's important to me that everyone's ideas are heard and considered."

Scenario: Your friend has been talking behind your back and spreading rumors about you.
Example: "I want to talk to you about something that's been bothering me. I heard that you've been saying some things about me that aren't true, and it's really been affecting our friendship. I value our relationship, and I think it's important that we're honest with each other and address this situation."

Scenario: You're in a disagreement with your sibling over sharing a household chore.
Example: "I understand that we may have different opinions on how to divvy up the laundry, but I think it's important that we both contribute evenly. Can we come up with a compromise that works for both of us?"

Remember, expressing yourself assertively is about standing up for yourself while respecting the other person. These scenarios demonstrate how you can effectively resolve conflict while maintaining healthy relationships.

So next time you find yourself in a disagreement, take a step back, put on your problem-solving hat, and remember that proactive conflict resolution is the key to maintaining your sanity, your relationships, and your precious heart.

35. Show Empathy and Compassion

Empathy means putting yourself in someone else's shoes and understanding how they feel. It's crucial to emotional intelligence because it helps us connect with others, build relationships, resolve conflicts, and respond more compassionately. Empathy is not about fixing the other person's problems but showing that you care and are willing to listen.

Imagine your best friend comes to you upset because they didn't do well on a test. You could respond with sympathy, saying something like, "That's too bad. I'm sorry you didn't do well." But empathy takes it a step further. You might say something like, "I know how frustrating it can be to work hard for something and not get the results you were hoping for. It's okay to feel disappointed, and I'm here for you."

See how empathy goes beyond just acknowledging the other person's feelings? It requires you to relate to their experience on a deeper level, validate their emotions, and offer support. When you respond with empathy, you make the other person feel seen and heard, which can help them feel less alone in their struggles.

Here is another scenario to show you what it would be like to respond with empathy.

Scenario: You were really excited to hang out with your best friend, but something unexpected came up, and you had to cancel. Now your friend is upset.

Example: "I know we had plans, and I'm sorry for canceling. I understand how much this meant to you. Can we reschedule when you're free and catch up on what we wanted to do?"

This response acknowledges your friend's feelings, takes responsibility for your actions, and expresses your willingness to make things right.

Remember: Empathy is not about minimizing the other person's feelings but rather about showing them that there is space for all of their emotions and that all of them are welcome.

36. Be Honest

My mother always said, "Honesty's the best policy". What she meant by this was that it's important to speak the truth, even when it's not the easiest thing to do. Honesty shows integrity and authenticity, and it helps us build a solid foundation of trust with others. Ditch the fibs and embrace the power of honesty. Be truthful in your words and actions, and you'll find that people respect and appreciate your genuine nature. Remember, honesty is not just about others; it's also about being true to yourself.

37. Recognize Toxic Friendships

Imagine you're walking through a dense forest surrounded by towering trees and vibrant foliage. The forest represents your life, which is filled with different relationships that shape who you are. As you explore, you come across a mesmerizing flower garden. Each flower represents a friend in your life, spreading beauty and positivity.

But among these beautiful blooms, there's a garden within the garden; an enchanting yet treacherous section. Here, the flowers appear striking at first glance, but their beauty hides a dangerous secret. These flowers are toxic friends.

Just as toxic flowers can harm your health, toxic friends can harm your emotional well-being. They might seem appealing and popular, but their true colors emerge when you spend more time with them. These friends often bring negativity and constant criticism into your life, leaving you feeling drained and unhappy.

Imagine a flower that steals the sunlight, refusing to let you grow and flourish. Toxic friends behave in a similar way. They overshadow your accomplishments, belittle your dreams, and make you doubt your worth. They thrive on drama, spreading gossip like invasive weeds and choking the positivity from your life.

But here's the thing: You have the power to choose. You can choose to nurture the flowers that bring joy, warmth, and support to your garden. Surrounding yourself with friends who understand, uplift, and inspire you is like cultivating a thriving, vibrant garden. These friends water your dreams, bask in your successes, and provide the shade of comfort during challenging times.

On the other hand, distancing yourself from toxic friends is like weeding your garden. It's not an easy task, but it's necessary for your growth and happiness. Just as you wouldn't let poisonous plants overtake your garden, you shouldn't let toxic friendships consume your life. As you remove them, you create space for new, healthier relationships to blossom.

Remember, the quality of your garden is determined by the flowers you choose to keep. Surround yourself with friends who celebrate your uniqueness, encourage your growth, and make you feel good about yourself. By doing so, you'll create a flourishing garden of friendships where you can truly thrive.

Setting Boundaries With Toxic Friends

Setting boundaries with toxic friends is crucial for your well-being. Here are some tips to help you establish and maintain healthy boundaries:

- **Recognize the signs.** First, identify the behaviors and patterns that make a friend toxic. Are they constantly putting you down, manipulating you, or disrespecting your boundaries? Understanding their negative impact on your life is the first step toward setting boundaries.
- **Reflect on your needs.** Take some time to reflect on what you need from your friendships. Consider your values, goals, and the kind of support you seek. This self-awareness will help you establish clear boundaries that align with your needs and values.
- **Communicate assertively.** When setting boundaries, it's important to communicate your needs clearly and assertively. I've mentioned it before, but it's worth saying again: Use "I" statements to express how their behavior affects you and what you need from them. For example, say, "I feel hurt when you make fun of me. I would appreciate it if you could refrain from making those comments in the future."
- **Be specific.** Clearly define the boundaries you want to set. Whether it's asking them not to share personal information without your consent or requesting that they respect your time and space, be specific about your expectations. This clarity helps prevent misunderstandings.
- **Stick to your boundaries.** Setting boundaries is only effective if you enforce them. If a toxic friend continues to disregard your boundaries, it may be necessary to distance yourself from that friendship. Remember that it's okay to prioritize your well-being and surround yourself with positive influences.

38. Foster Family Connections

I love that the expression "family" means that no one gets left behind or gets forgotten.

Fostering strong family connections is essential for building a support system that lasts a lifetime. When you feel connected to your family members, you are more likely to have a sense of belonging and security, which can give you the strength and motivation to succeed in all areas of life.

But how can you create deep, meaningful connections with your family members in today's world, where everyone seems so busy and distracted by technology and other responsibilities?

One way to start is by making time for each other. It can be as simple as having a weekly family dinner or movie night or planning fun activities together like a family game night. When you spend time with your loved ones, you show them that they are a priority in your life.

Another effective way to strengthen family connections is by creating traditions. This can be as simple as baking cookies together every holiday season or taking an annual summer trip to the beach. Traditions offer a way to connect and create a shared history that can keep families feeling close, even across generations.

Lastly, fostering family connections requires forgiveness and the willingness to work through possible conflicts. No family is perfect, and inevitably, conflicts will arise. However, if you can approach conflicts with a desire to understand and work through the issue together, you can strengthen your bonds and grow closer as a result.

So love your people. Show them that they matter. There's really nothing quite like that feeling of having people around who you know have your back, and vice versa.

39. Say "Thank You" More Often

When was the last time you said thank you to someone? Thank you to the tutor who gave you study tips to ace your science test, or to the cashier who helped you and your mom bag your groceries? I think we often tend to underestimate the power of a thank you. It seems like a small gesture, but it can actually have a big impact on both you and the person you're thanking.

For starters, saying thank you can boost your mood and help you feel more positive. When you express gratitude, it can activate the release of feel-good chemicals in your brain, like dopamine and oxytocin. This is why you might notice that you feel happier and more content after showing appreciation to someone else.

But it's not just about you—saying thank you can benefit the other person in numerous ways. Taking the time to recognize someone's efforts shows that you value and appreciate them. This can make them feel more confident and validated, which can have a ripple effect on their day.

Unfortunately, we live in a world that often encourages us to take things for granted instead of expressing appreciation. Our busy lives, coupled with the constant barrage of notifications and distractions, can make it easy to forget the small gestures of kindness that people do for us each day. But it's important to pause and recognize these moments because they add up to make a big difference in our overall happiness and well-being.

So, the next time you're tempted to rush past someone helping you or overlook a kind gesture, try to slow down and offer a heartfelt thank you instead. You'll be amazed at how much of a difference it can make. And who knows? Your gratitude might just inspire someone else to spread kindness and positivity in their own way.

40. Learn to Forgive and Let Go of Grudges

Forgiveness is rarely about the other person because they rarely ever change. It's all about you because you have the power to change for yourself.

Forgiveness is a lot like tackling a messy wound, but instead of bandages and antiseptics, we're dealing with emotions and relationships. Picture this: You accidentally cut your finger while chopping vegetables. Ouch! It stings, and you can see it starting to bleed and swelling up. If you just leave it be, thinking, *Eh, it'll heal on its own*, you're in for a world of trouble.

When someone hurts us, whether it's a friend, a family member, or even a romantic partner, it's like a wound that digs deep into our hearts. The pain is real, and it's totally understandable to feel angry, betrayed, or hurt. But here's the thing: Holding onto those negative emotions only prolongs the agony and messes with the healing process.

Imagine your cut finger getting all gunky and infected because you didn't clean it. Yikes! Not a pretty sight, right? Well, the same goes for holding grudges. When we let anger and resentment fester inside us, they can infect our thoughts, our relationships, and even our overall well-being. We become trapped in a cycle of negativity, unable to move forward.

But guess what? Just as you clean a wound to prevent infection, forgiveness is like a soothing balm you apply to your emotional wounds. It's not about pretending that the pain doesn't exist or brushing it under the rug. Forgiveness is acknowledging the hurt, facing it head-on, and actively working toward letting it go. It's a powerful act of self-care. By forgiving, you're taking back control of your emotions and refusing to let them consume you.

Sure, forgiveness can be tough. It's not an overnight miracle cure, just like a wound doesn't magically disappear the moment you clean it. It takes time, effort, and sometimes even support from others. But the rewards are immense.

Imagine the relief you feel when your cut finger finally starts to heal and you can use it without wincing in pain. Well, that's the feeling forgiveness brings to your heart and mind. It allows you to move forward, to rebuild trust, and to create a more positive and fulfilling life.

A few final reminders on forgiveness:

- Holding onto anger and resentment only weighs you down. Forgiveness is like releasing a heavy burden you carry on your shoulders. So, take a deep breath and let go of that grudge. You'll feel lighter, I promise!
- Forgiving someone doesn't mean you're letting them off the hook or condoning their actions. It's about freeing yourself from the negativity that comes with holding onto pain. Forgiveness is a gift you give yourself, not just the other person.
- We're all human, and we all make mistakes. Maybe the other person didn't mean to hurt you, or perhaps they're struggling with their own demons. Understanding their perspective can help you find compassion and make forgiveness a little easier.
- Practice self-forgiveness. Oh boy, this one can be tough! Remember, we all make mistakes, including ourselves. Be kind to yourself and forgive your own shortcomings. Treat yourself with the same compassion you'd extend to others. Self-forgiveness is a vital part of personal growth.

41. Be Open-Minded

Open-mindedness, I'm sure, is a phrase you've probably heard your teachers using a lot, but what exactly does it mean, and what traits does an open-minded person have? Well, allow me to break it down for you.

Pretend for a moment that you're at a buffet, and all you see is one big plate of broccoli. Now, if you're not a fan of these little green trees, you might be tempted to turn up your nose and declare them the enemy of your taste buds. But hold on a second! Being open-minded means giving them a chance, even if they don't immediately scream "delicious!"

Open-mindedness is all about being willing to consider new ideas, perspectives, and possibilities. An open-minded person is like a sponge, ready to soak up knowledge and experiences without judgment or preconceived notions.

It's about having an eagerness to learn something new. To appreciate the beauty of different cultures, beliefs, and backgrounds. It's also about listening. Open-minded people don't just hear words; they actively listen, seeking to understand rather than jumping to conclusions. They are willing to adapt and change perspective when presented with new information.

So, the next time you hear that phrase, embrace it with open arms (and an open mind), and get ready to embark on an incredible journey of discovery.

42. Respect Yourself

You are at this stage in your life when you are constantly discovering who you are and who you want to become. It is during this time that learning to respect yourself becomes much more important. While the concept of self-respect may seem abstract or intangible, it is, in fact, an essential attribute that will shape your character, relationships, and overall success.

First and foremost, self-respect is about recognizing your worth and value as a person. It is understanding that you deserve to be treated with kindness, dignity, and compassion by both yourself and others. When you respect yourself, you set healthy boundaries and refuse to settle for less than you deserve.

Self-respect empowers you to set realistic goals, work toward them, and persevere even in the face of setbacks. It enables you to believe in your abilities and have confidence in your decisions.

It is also about prioritizing all aspects of your mental, physical, and emotional health, which influences how you present yourself to the world. It is reflected in your appearance, behavior, and the way you carry yourself. When you respect yourself, you take pride in your appearance, not because you want approval from others but because you want to feel good about yourself. You understand the importance of dressing appropriately for different occasions and presenting yourself in a manner that reflects your values and beliefs.

In a world that often puts pressure on you to conform or seek validation from others, remember that your self-respect is your greatest ally.

43. Seek out Healthy Relationships

Healthy relationships are the kind that bring out the best in you, but are not afraid to hold you accountable. They challenge you, but they don't force you to hide the essence of who you are.

First and foremost, it's essential to understand that a healthy relationship is based on mutual respect. This means treating each other as equals, valuing each other's opinions and feelings, and being considerate of each other's needs and boundaries. Healthy relationships don't manipulate, control, or emotionally abuse the other. They are gentle and kind.

Being able to express yourself honestly and openly, and listening to your friend or partner with empathy and understanding, is vital to building a strong foundation.

In a healthy relationship, you can share your thoughts, feelings, hopes, and fears without fear of judgment or rejection. You can also work through conflicts together without resorting to name-calling, shouting, or verbal attacks.

My grandmother used to tell me that you don't teach people how you want to be treated in relationships, you *show* them. What she meant was that you can't expect someone to treat you a certain way if you don't set an example and show them how it's done.

In relationships, it's not just about what you say but also about how you act. You can tell someone that you want to be treated with respect, kindness, and consideration, but if you don't demonstrate those qualities yourself, your words will likely fall on deaf ears. When you treat your friend or partner the way you want to be treated, you're also setting a standard for the kind of behavior you're willing to accept. You're letting them know that certain behaviors, such as disrespect and manipulation, are not acceptable and will not be tolerated. It's ultimately about creating a safe and supportive space where both of you can thrive.

44. Set and Enforce Boundaries

Where emotions run wild, things can get a little messy. This is especially true when it comes to romantic relationships. As a teenage girl, you might not feel the need to dive too deeply into the world of romantic relationships just yet, but it's valuable to be prepared for what the future may hold.

Sometimes, you meet someone, sparks fly, and before you know it, you're head over heels. But as exciting as those early days can be, it's important to remember that setting boundaries and honoring mutual respect and consent are crucial to building healthy, fulfilling relationships.

Boundaries are all about protecting your physical and emotional safety and ensuring you feel comfortable and respected. If you're not sure what your boundaries are, take some time to reflect on what's important to you. Maybe you're not comfortable being intimate on the first date, or maybe you have certain expectations when it comes to communication or spending time together. Whatever it is, make sure you communicate those boundaries clearly and respectfully.

It's easy to get caught up in the excitement of a new relationship, but it's important to remember that both partners deserve to be heard and valued. That means actively listening to your partner's thoughts and feelings and treating them with kindness and consideration. And if there's ever a disagreement or misunderstanding, remember that it's okay to take a step back and have a mature, respectful conversation about it.

Last but certainly not least, consent is key. Whether you're talking about physical intimacy or just hanging out together, both partners should feel comfortable and enthusiastic about what's happening. If anyone ever tries to pressure or coerce you into doing something you're uncomfortable with, feel free to shut that down real quick. Just remember, communication, respect, and consent never go out of style.

Rise and Shine

Embracing Growth and Bouncing Back From Challenges

Navigating the landscape of your dreams can be quite a humbling experience. You take a few confident steps forward, only to fall down. You get back up and start making progress, then find another obstacle waiting for you a couple of miles ahead.

It's like trying to hike up Mount Everest with no map or compass. It's tough, and it's unpredictable.

Some days, it feels like you're making all the progress in the world. You're crushing your goals, ticking off your to-do list, and feeling darn proud of yourself. And then, out of nowhere, life throws another challenge your way, and you're knocked back down to the bottom of the mountain. It's frustrating, isn't it? But here's the thing: The journey to achieving your dreams is never a straight line. It's full of twists and turns, ups and downs, and unexpected obstacles. And while that can be challenging, it's also what makes the journey so rewarding.

Think about it. If achieving your dreams was easy, it wouldn't be nearly as fulfilling. It's the challenges you face, the setbacks you overcome, and the obstacles you conquer that make the destination worth it.

So, the next time you feel like you're taking two steps forward and one step back, remember that it's all part of the process. Don't beat yourself up for not being where you want to be just yet. Celebrate the progress you've made so far, take a deep breath, and keep on climbing. Keep pushing and keep dreaming. The view from the top is going to be oh so sweet.

45. Be Curious

Smart girls ask questions. They're interested in the world, they're daring, and they're unafraid to be bold.

I suspect every time you ask a question in class, at least three other students want to know the answer but are too scared to put their hand up and ask. When you ask those questions, you're satisfying not just your own curiosity but that of those around you—it's like giving a voice to the voiceless, which is super empowering if you think about it.

Being curious shows that you are engaged and interested in the world around you. People—not just your teachers—love it when you ask them questions, especially if it's a topic they are interested in. Every question you ask is an opportunity to learn and grow. Remember, even some of the greatest minds started with simple questions like "Why does an apple fall from a tree?" (Thanks, Sir Isaac Newton.)

Embrace that curiosity and let it be the very thing that carries you through life. Be the girl who raises her hand and fearlessly asks, "Why?" "How?" "What if?" Be the kind of girl who inspires others to join this brilliant quest for knowledge.

46. Try New Things

So you're comfortably nestled in your little bubble, surrounded by familiar faces, routines, and experiences. It's pretty much like you're living in a cozy blanket fort, safe and secure. But here's the thing: Growth doesn't happen inside that fort. It happens when you muster up the courage to step outside and explore the vast unknown.

Smart girls know that when they allow themselves to be exposed to things outside their norm, they open the door to endless possibilities. It's like stepping into a magical wardrobe and finding a whole new world waiting for you. Whether it's trying a new hobby, exploring a different culture, or challenging your beliefs, that is where the magic happens.

Think about it: When you try something new, you're pushing the boundaries of what you thought was possible. You're expanding your horizons, gaining new perspectives, and discovering hidden talents you never knew existed. It's like unlocking a secret level in the game of life, where growth and personal development are the ultimate rewards.

And yes, it can be downright terrifying. The fear of the unknown can be paralyzing, making you want to retreat back to the safety of your comfort zone.

When you challenge yourself and embrace the unfamiliar, you become stronger and more resilient. You learn to adapt, think on your feet, and overcome obstacles. You become the hero of your own story, conquering fears and achieving things you never thought possible.

So, be brave, fierce, and fabulous, and watch yourself bloom into the incredible person you are meant to be.

47. Take Calculated Risks

I've always been quite cautious and resistant to taking risks. I followed all the rules and hated stepping outside my comfort zone. But in my freshman year, I realized playing it safe was stopping me from learning, growing, and having new experiences. I decided to start taking more strategic, calculated risks. My first challenge was auditioning for the lead role in the school musical.

I was terrified. What if I forgot the lines or completely messed up? But I wrote down the potential risks and rewards and realized I had a lot more to gain than lose by putting myself out there. After a ton of rehearsing, I nailed the nerve-wracking audition. And guess what? I got the lead role!

So, my guidance to you is to look for opportunities to take risks, even when success isn't guaranteed. Ask yourself, what's the worst that can happen? Then weigh the potential downsides against all that you could gain if you proceeded.

Whether it's raising your hand more in class or trying out for a competitive team, taking calculated risks and putting yourself out there always leads to growth. Sure, some attempts don't pan out perfectly. But by reflecting on risks that don't work out, you learn lessons for next time.

48. Set SMART Goals

You are allowed to chase your dreams! In fact, you are not just allowed but encouraged to be loud, unapologetic, and brave about the things that make your heart beat faster.

Imagine a world where everyone dared to chase their dreams fearlessly. A world filled with individuals unafraid to step out of their comfort zones, take risks, and embrace the unknown. It would be a world bursting with creativity, innovation, and endless possibilities. So why not be a part of that world? Let your heart race with excitement, let your spirit soar with passion, and let your dreams be the fuel that propels you forward.

But, remember, to make your dreams a reality, you have to have an action plan. You need SMART goals.

Tips for Setting SMART Goals

- **Specific:** When setting goals, be as specific as a well-crafted treasure map. Avoid vague or ambiguous goals that leave you wandering aimlessly like a lost pirate. Instead, set clear targets that guide you directly to your desired treasure chest. For example, instead of saying, "I want to exercise more," say, "I will jog for 30 minutes every morning before breakfast."
- **Measurable:** Make your goals measurable, like a talented baker who follows a recipe with precise measurements. This way, you can track your progress and know exactly when you've baked the perfect cake. For instance, if your goal is to improve your guitar skills, you could set a measurable goal such as, "I will learn to play two new songs by the end of the month."

- **Achievable:** Ensure your goals are achievable. Avoid setting goals that are too far-fetched or unrealistic because that will only lead to frustration and disappointment. Instead, choose goals that challenge you but are within your reach. For example, if you're learning a new language, setting a goal to have a basic conversation with a native speaker within six months is more achievable than aiming to become fluent in just one month.
- **Relevant:** Make your goals relevant. Ensure that your goals align with your broader aspirations and are meaningful to you. Consider how achieving the goal will contribute to your personal or professional growth. For instance, if you're aiming to run for something like the student body leadership role, setting a goal to enhance your leadership skills would be relevant.
- **Time-bound:** Set time-bound goals, like a thrilling countdown to a New Year's Eve celebration. Establishing deadlines creates a sense of urgency and helps you stay focused and motivated. Without a specific time frame, goals may lose their luster and get lost in the vast sea of possibilities. For example, instead of saying, "I will learn how to play the guitar someday," set a time-bound goal like, "I will learn how to play six chords on the guitar within the next six months."

By setting SMART goals, you can channel your focus on what's important, maintain motivation, and hold yourself accountable, setting you on the path to success. So why not try giving SMART goals a go?

49. Ask for Feedback

Feedback is a necessary part of growth, but it's not always the most pleasant experience. When you don't receive the kind of feedback you want to hear, it can be a hard pill to swallow. But learning to accept constructive criticism will do wonders for you.

When someone gives you feedback, your initial reaction might be to become defensive or dismissive. But I encourage you to step back and truly listen to what the person is saying. Consider their perspective and try to see things from their point of view. Who knows? They might have some valuable insights you never would have discovered on your own.

Another thing to keep in mind is that not all feedback is created equal. Some feedback may be more constructive and helpful than others, so it's important to filter out the noise and focus on the feedback that will make the most significant impact on your growth. And here's a little secret: The harshest feedback is often the most valuable. As much as it may sting, it's usually the feedback that will make you grow the most.

But at the end of the day, it's up to you how you choose to receive and apply feedback. You can choose to ignore it, become defensive, or take it to heart and use it to fuel your growth. It takes courage to face your weaknesses head-on, but when you do, you'll become stronger, wiser, and more confident.

So, the next time someone gives you feedback, take a deep breath and embrace it with an open mind and heart. See it as an opportunity to learn and grow, and remember that even the most successful people in the world had to face their fair share of criticism to get to where they are today.

50. Explore New Cultures

Traveling allows you to immerse yourself in different cultures, walk the streets of foreign cities, and connect with people from all walks of life. It's like a crash course in empathy and understanding as you witness firsthand the beauty and diversity in our world. But if travel isn't in the cards at the moment, that's okay. There's a delicious alternative that will transport your taste buds to far-off lands: trying new cuisines. Food is a universal language, and exploring different culinary traditions is like taking a culinary journey around the globe. From spicy curries to savory dumplings, each bite is an opportunity to experience a new culture's flavors, traditions, and history.

51. Read Widely and Often

Reading plays a vital role in your transition into adulthood and beyond. Think of the wise words by Dr. Suess: "The more you read, the more things you will know. The more you will learn, the more places you will go." Reading allows you to explore new ideas, perspectives, and cultures, broadening your understanding of the world around you. Whether it's non-fiction, fiction, or something in between, go ahead and engage with written material. Reading will help you become a more well-rounded individual better equipped to navigate life's challenges.

52. Celebrate Achievements

Celebrating your achievements, no matter how big or small, is a vital aspect of your journey through adolescence. I'm not talking about bragging or being boastful, but recognizing your hard work and accomplishments and giving yourself the credit you deserve.

As a teenager, it's easy to focus on your goals and aspirations, but taking the time to acknowledge and celebrate what you've accomplished along the way is equally crucial.

Why? Because celebrating achievements boosts your self-esteem and confidence. And don't we all want a little more of that? Recognizing your successes, whether they involve academics, sports, hobbies, or personal growth, reinforces your belief in your capabilities. It reminds you that your hard work pays off and that you're capable of reaching your goals.

When you celebrate your progress and achievements, it inspires you to keep pushing forward and striving for even greater accomplishments.

Remember, celebrating achievements doesn't have to be extravagant or public; it can be as simple as a personal pat on the back or sharing your success with a close friend or family member. By doing so, you'll cultivate a habit of recognizing and appreciating your growth and accomplishments, which will serve you well as you continue to mature into a confident and capable young woman.

53. Be a Critical Thinker

Critical thinking is about sharpening your mind, honing your analytical skills, and questioning everything that comes your way. It's not about being skeptical for the sake of it but rather about seeking truth, understanding, and making informed decisions.

Why is critical thinking so important? Well, let me break it down for you. In a world filled with information overload and fake news, being a critical thinker is like having a truth detector. It helps you sift through the noise, separate fact from fiction, and make sense of the chaos.

But it doesn't stop there. It also empowers you to become an active participant in your own life. It's like having a compass that guides you through the maze of choices and challenges. It allows you to evaluate options, weigh consequences, and make decisions that align with your values and goals.

But here's the catch: It is something that requires work. It requires effort, patience, and a willingness to embrace uncertainty. It means you have to be open to different perspectives, even if they challenge your own beliefs. It's about being comfortable with ambiguity and embracing the discomfort of not having all the answers.

Ask questions, seek evidence, and challenge the world around you. Be the one who doesn't settle for surface-level understanding but dives deep into the root of things.

54. Learn From Others

Learning from the wisdom and experiences of others is a valuable practice that can greatly enhance your personal growth and development—not to mention, save you a lot of time.

Observing and listening to those who have walked the path before you allows you to access a vast wealth of knowledge and insights. Their wisdom can give you the guidance you need, helping you avoid potential pitfalls and make wiser decisions. Their experiences are what help you gain perspective, broaden your horizons, and spark new ideas.

By humbling yourself and acknowledging that you don't have all the answers (which is okay, by the way) and being open to learning from others, you can accelerate your own learning journey and navigate life's challenges with greater wisdom and grace.

55. Persevere When Things Get Tough

When things get really tough, the default can often be to run. To give up, because why is it worth it if you have to struggle so much, right? But you know what? It's that grit, that tenacity, that's going to get you much further. Nothing worthwhile comes easy. Perseverance is the key to unlocking true growth and progress.

When faced with obstacles or setbacks, it can be tempting to throw in the towel and give up. But by pushing through the tough times, you build resilience, strength, and character. It's in those moments of struggle that you have the opportunity to learn and grow the most.

Here are some tips to help keep you going when the going gets tough:

- **Stay focused on your goal.** Remind yourself of the ultimate goal you are working toward. Visualize the end result and keep it in mind to stay motivated.
- **Break it down.** When faced with a difficult situation, break it down into smaller, manageable tasks. This will help you stay focused and prevent you from becoming too overwhelmed by feelings.
- **Don't go at it alone.** Sharing your struggles with others can help alleviate the burden and provide fresh perspectives.
- **Embrace failure as a learning opportunity.** Understand that setbacks and failures are a natural part of any journey. Instead of letting them discourage you, view them as opportunities for growth and learning. Analyze what went wrong, learn from it, and adapt your approach.
- **Cultivate a positive mindset.** Believe in your ability to overcome challenges. Adopt a growth mindset, understanding that with effort and perseverance, you can develop new skills and improve your situation.
- **Be consistent.** Even if progress seems slow, take small steps toward your goal every day. Consistent effort, no matter how small, will eventually lead to significant progress.
- **Reflect.** Remember the reasons why you started this journey in the first place. Reconnect with your passion and purpose, as it will fuel your determination to persevere through tough times.

56. Be Open to Change

Flexibility and adaptability are important in the pursuit of your dreams. Flexibility is like a graceful dancer, allowing you to bend and sway with the challenges that come your way. It's the ability to adjust your plans, expectations, and even your mindset when faced with unexpected detours. Instead of rigidly sticking to a predetermined path, flexibility allows you to explore alternative routes, embrace new opportunities, and find creative solutions to problems.

Adaptability, on the other hand, is like a chameleon, blending seamlessly into different environments. It's the skill to acclimate yourself to unfamiliar circumstances, whether it's changing schools, learning new skills, or making new friends. Adaptability allows you to thrive in the face of uncertainty, to embrace change as an opportunity for growth, and to evolve along with your dreams.

Together, flexibility and adaptability create a dynamic duo that helps you navigate the twists and turns of being a teenager. They ensure that you don't get stuck in rigid expectations but instead remain open to the unexpected possibilities that may arise. They empower you to embrace change, to pivot when necessary, and to approach obstacles with resilience and creativity.

57. Embrace Failure

Let's face it, trying something new is scarier than watching *Final Destination*. The easy thing to do when things don't go your way is to give up and go home. But my advice that I hope you really take to heart is to not allow failure to deter you from pursuing your passions; use it as a learning opportunity and keep pushing yourself, just like these successful women did.

- **J.K. Rowling**, the genius behind the Harry Potter series, faced a barrage of rejections from publishers. Her unwavering persistence and self-belief transformed her into a globally celebrated author.
- **Sara Blakely**, the founder of Spanx, a billion-dollar undergarment brand, encountered numerous failures and rejections while launching her revolutionary product. Her steadfast determination and belief in her vision ultimately led her to unparalleled success.
- **Vera Wang** started her journey as a figure skater but fell short of making the Olympic team. She transitioned into the fashion industry, initially grappling with criticism and doubt. Today, she's a renowned fashion designer with a global presence.

The lesson here is clear: Failure is not a dead-end but a stepping stone to greatness. Like my father used to say, *"If you're not winning, you're learning."* Each setback imparts resilience, determination, and the significance of persistence. It's in these challenging moments that you evolve, adapt, and discover your true potential. Don't let fear hold you back; let it fuel your determination to continue striving, growing, and ultimately achieving your dreams.

58. Keep Learning

I get it, you're already a student, and the last thing you want is a lecture about more learning. But here's the twist—we're not talking about extra assignments or textbooks. We're diving into the exciting world of mindset, where the way you approach learning can change your life.

So, let's talk about two mindsets: the growth mindset and the fixed mindset.

A **growth mindset** is the belief that abilities and intelligence can be developed with effort and learning. If you have a growth mindset you embrace challenges, persist through obstacles, and see failure as a stepping stone toward improvement. For example, when you face a difficult math problem and keep working on it until you understand, you're exercising a growth mindset. A growth mindset is always fluid, changing, expanding, and improving,

In contrast, a **fixed mindset** is the belief that abilities and intelligence are fixed traits, limiting the potential for change. If you have a fixed mindset, you tend to avoid challenges, give up easily when faced with difficulties, and view failure as a reflection of your abilities. For instance, if you avoid learning a new language because you believe you'll never be good at it, you're operating with a fixed mindset.

Take a look at this table and consider which statements ring true for you.

Fixed Mindset	Growth Mindset
I don't like to try new things because it's uncomfortable.	I enjoy trying new things and stepping out of my comfort zone.
I don't think that failure is an option for me.	I see failure as a necessary part of the learning process.
I compare myself to others and feel inferior.	I compare myself to my previous self and focus on my own progress.
I believe that my potential is limited by my circumstances.	I believe that my potential is limitless and that I can overcome any obstacles with hard work and dedication.
I think that asking for help is a sign of weakness.	I think that asking for help is a sign of strength and an opportunity to learn from others.
I believe that intelligence is innate and cannot be developed.	I believe that intelligence can be developed through hard work and dedication.
I have learned all I need to know.	There are still so many things I want to learn.
I am limited by my past failures and mistakes.	I embrace challenges as opportunities to learn and grow.
I give up easily when faced with obstacles or setbacks.	I persevere through obstacles and setbacks and use them as opportunities to learn and grow.

Think about which mindset you currently have? Is it the mindset that will help you achieve all your goals and dreams?

The bottom line is, the more you learn, the more you grow, both as an individual and as a positive force in the world. So, keep on learning, embrace a growth mindset, and you'll be amazed at what you can achieve.

Love Your Reflection

Embracing Body Confidence

Your body is your home, did you know that? It's this vessel that's carrying you through life's thick and thin. It's what allows you to experience the delight and messiness of being a person alive. Do you love yours, or are you constantly trying to shame yours?

In a society that often presents unrealistic standards of beauty and perfection, it is no wonder that so many of us find ourselves trapped in a never-ending cycle of self-doubt and self-criticism.

But here's the truth: Your body, with all its imperfections and uniqueness, is a masterpiece. Every curve, scar, and freckle tells a story, a testament to the experiences and journeys you have undertaken. Instead of fixating on perceived flaws, how about you embrace and celebrate the beauty of your body?

Loving your body does not mean conforming to societal ideals or striving for a specific shape or size. It means accepting and appreciating your body for what it is, acknowledging its resilience, and cherishing the countless ways it supports and enables you to live a fulfilling life. Whether it's the ability to dance, run, hug loved ones, or simply experience the world through your senses, your body is the vehicle that allows you to engage fully in life's pleasures.

59. Move Your Body

When was the last time you did something to help you feel good about your body? When was the last time you celebrated the strength and capabilities of your body? Movement matters. Not just because it's good for our bodies, but because it's good for our souls, too. Think about how good you often feel after a good ol' sweat session. You feel incredible, right?

I think so many of us are conditioned to believe that we should move and exercise as a way to change our bodies instead of as a way to declare our bold, undying love for them. Right here, you and I are breaking and changing that narrative because the joy of movement is movement.

Here are some tips on moving your body for the joy of it:

- **Dance like no one's watching.** Put on your favorite tunes and let loose! Don't worry about looking silly or getting the moves right. Just have fun and enjoy the feeling of moving to the beat.
- **Treat your body.** After a good workout or dance session, treat your body to some self-care. Take a relaxing bath, get a massage, or stretch out your muscles with some gentle yoga.
- **Connect with others.** Join a dance class, a sports team, or a hiking group. Moving with others can be a great way to connect and make new friends while enjoying the benefits of physical activity.
- **Keep it playful.** Remember that movement doesn't have to be serious or strenuous. Consider adding some playfulness to your practice with activities like hula hooping, jumping rope, or playing tag with your friends.

60. Develop a Healthy Relationship With Food

Food is not the enemy. I know that diet culture tends to send us those messages that make it actually feel like it is, but it's not. Food is fuel. It's sustenance. This is your reminder that you don't have to go for the lower calorie option. You don't have to skip meals just because you ate a little too much yesterday or because you had an extra piece of cake. You don't have to eat less just because your friend has a smaller body than you do. Our bodies' needs are not the same, so it makes sense why our needs would be different as well. This is where intuitive eating comes in.

Basically, intuitive eating is a way of nourishing your body and soul while ditching the restrictive rules and guilt surrounding food. It's all about listening to your body's natural signals, such as hunger and fullness cues, and eating accordingly. Intuitive eating encourages you to savor and enjoy the food you eat without feeling guilty about it.

Here are a few tips to help you practicing intuitive eating.

- **Put aside the diet mentality.** Say bye-bye to counting calories, tracking macros, and following strict meal plans. These can lead to an unhealthy relationship with food and your body.
- **Tune into your body.** Pay attention to your hunger and fullness cues. Are you really hungry or just bored? Do you feel satisfied or stuffed to the brim?
- **Get rid of food guilt**. Guilt is not a helpful or productive emotion. Instead of dwelling on the "bad" food choices you made, focus on nourishing your body with the next meal or snack.
- **Trust yourself.** You are the expert on your body. Trust that you know what's best for yourself and that you can make choices that support your health and well-being.

61. Embrace Your Body

Learning to love and embrace your body for all that it is and does for you is the best thing that you'll ever do for yourself. Bodies aren't perfect, and they're not supposed to be, but they're beautiful in their imperfections. It's important to understand that every individual is unique, and so is their body. Comparing yourself to others only creates unnecessary pressure and self-doubt. Instead, focus on what your body can do and be grateful for it.

Learning to love your body also involves taking care of it. This means fueling it with nutritious foods, staying hydrated, and exercising regularly. It's not about achieving a certain body shape or size but rather taking care of your body and giving it what it needs to thrive.

Moreover, embracing your body involves accepting and celebrating all of its features, including so-called flaws. Instead of feeling embarrassed or ashamed of scars or that birthmark you have, recognize them as unique parts of your body that tell a story.

Finally, it's important to surround yourself with positivity and avoid negative body talk from yourself or others. Be mindful of the words you use when talking about your body or others' bodies, and strive for kindness and compassion. The words you say will always have a bigger impact than you think, so when and where you can, choose kindness, choose grace, and choose tenderness in your words; that is something that you certainly won't regret.

62. Know Your Worth in the Real World

It's pretty cool to get gushing admiration from your online followers and all, but it's important to remember that your worth goes beyond social media likes. In a world where validation is often sought through virtual approval, you have to understand that your value lies in your unique qualities, talents, and accomplishments.

Likes and followers can be fleeting, and basing your self-worth on them can lead to a constant need for validation. Instead, focus on building genuine connections and nurturing your passions. Engage in activities that bring you joy and fulfillment, whether it's playing an instrument, writing, or volunteering.

Social media is really just a curated version of reality, and comparing yourself to others based on likes can be damaging to your self-esteem. Embrace your individuality and celebrate your own journey. Your value comes from within, not from the number of likes on a post. Don't ever forget that.

63. Be Kind to Yourself

I know how hard it can be to feel good about your body with all the pressure out there. But listen up—your body is amazing just how it is! I used to compare myself constantly too, but it only made me feel worse. Now I know every body is different, and that's something to celebrate!

Don't let anyone else make you feel bad about your body or your looks—real beauty comes from within. Focus on appreciating what your body can do—it's strong, creative, and moves you through life.

It's okay to have off days where you don't feel your best, just don't beat yourself up. Treat your body with the kindness and respect it deserves. And when those negative thoughts creep in, replace them with positive truths—like you are beautiful, capable, and whole. Your body is wonderful because it's yours!

Dream Big, Work Hard

Mapping Your Path to Success

If you're the smart girl I think you are, I know you've got huge dreams brewing in that creative mind of yours. Visions of who you want to become, how you want to change the world, the grand adventures you want to go on. I'm telling you—don't let anyone dim that spark inside you. Your dreams matter. But here's the thing: Dreams without hard work are just wishful thinking. To achieve greatness, you've got to be willing to put in the effort.

Is it going to be easy? Nope. Will you want to give up some days? Probably. But anything truly rewarding takes dedication. Think of mastering a new skill like learning an instrument. At first, your fingers ache, you want to throw your sheet music across the room, and it seems impossible that you'll ever play a song fluidly. But with practice, patience, and persistence, you slowly improve. And when you finally perform a beautiful melody, you realize—that's why you don't give up.

But it starts with a first step, and the commitment to keep going. Arm yourself with passion, grit, and purpose. Make plans, set goals, work hard. You'll stumble, you'll make mistakes—learn from them, get back up, and keep striving.

You are capable of achieving extraordinary things. But you've got to dream big AND work hard. Luck favors the bold. Fortune favors the brave. Now go out there, and make those dreams happen.

64. Dream Big

You are allowed to envision a future that surpasses your wildest expectations, and you can be daring enough to chase after it with passion and determination. When you dream big, you ignite a fire within you that fuels your ambitions and propels you forward.

Think about it: The world is full of incredible stories of people who dared to dream big. They defied the odds, pushed boundaries, and achieved greatness. From inventors and artists to athletes and entrepreneurs, they all started with a dream.

So, why not you? Why not dream big and believe in the limitless possibilities that lie ahead? Allow your imagination to run wild and visualize the life you desire. Set audacious goals that excite and challenge you. Break free from the confines of what seems possible and dare to think beyond the ordinary.

But dreaming big is not enough. Achieving them is about taking action, stepping outside of your comfort zone, and persevering through obstacles. It requires dedication, hard work, and resilience. It may not always be an easy path, but the journey toward your big dreams is where you'll discover your true potential and grow in ways you never thought possible.

Believe in yourself, trust the process, and remember that the biggest dreams often lead to the most incredible adventures.

65. Develop Good Study Habits

Picture this: It's the night before a big exam, and you find yourself frantically flipping through pages, trying to cram as much information as possible into your tired brain. Sound familiar? But what if I told you that there's a better way? Developing good study habits not only helps you retain information more effectively but also reduces stress and sets you up for success in the long run.

You can't get that A+ if you have the study habits of a chronic procrastinator. So, what exactly are the secrets to unlocking smarter studying? Well, let's have a look:

- **Have a Dedicated Study Space.** Find a quiet, well-lit area where you can focus without distractions. Whether it's a corner of your room, a library, or a cozy coffee shop, having a designated study space helps signal to your brain that it's time to get down to business.
- **Understand Your Learning Style.** Everyone has different ways of absorbing and retaining information. Experiment with different study techniques to find what works best for you. Are you a visual learner? Try creating mind maps or using flashcards. Do you learn better through auditory cues? Consider recording your notes and listening to them later. Understanding your learning style will make your studying more effective and enjoyable.
- **Give Yourself Brain Breaks.** It may seem counterintuitive, but taking short breaks during study sessions can enhance your productivity. Our brains need time to rest and process information. Try the Pomodoro Technique, where you work for 25 minutes, then take a 5-minute break. Repeat this cycle a few times, and reward yourself with a longer break. You'll be amazed at how refreshed and focused you feel.
- **Stay Organized.** Keep your study materials, notes, and resources organized. Invest in a planner or use digital tools to keep track of deadlines, assignments, and important dates. Having a structured system helps alleviate stress and ensures you stay on top of your workload.

66. Set Academic Goals

Imagine waking up each day with a clear purpose, knowing exactly what you want to achieve at school, and having a plan to get there. Setting academic goals is like mapping out your journey to success. It gives you direction and motivation. If you're not sure how to start, I've got you covered.

First, think about what you want to achieve academically. Maybe you want to boost your grades, excel in a specific subject, or earn a scholarship. Take a moment to reflect on your aspirations and identify where you want to focus. A clear vision will guide your goal-setting process.

Make your goals specific and measurable. Instead of saying, "I want to do better in math," aim for something like, "I want to raise my math grade by one letter grade by the end of the semester." This makes it easier to track your progress and adjust as needed.

Once you've defined your goals, it's time to create an action plan. Big goals can sometimes feel overwhelming, so break them down into smaller, manageable milestones. Develop a timeline with short-term goals that lead to your ultimate academic objectives. Identify the steps you need to take to reach each milestone and allocate your time and resources wisely. Consider what support or resources you might need, whether it's tutoring, study groups, or extra materials. Having a well-structured plan will help you stay focused and on track.

Regularly check your progress and celebrate your achievements, no matter how small. This keeps you motivated and feeling good about your accomplishments. Be open to adjusting your goals as you go along—it's okay to change your mind or adapt to new circumstances.

With a solid plan and a clear vision, you'll be well on your way to achieving your academic goals. Remember to be flexible, stay motivated, and keep moving forward.

Goal Setting Template (Example)

1. Define your vision

Academic Dream: (e.g., Graduate with honors, get into a specific college)

Focus Areas: (e.g., Improve grades, earn a scholarship, excel in specific subjects)

2. Set Specific and Measurable Goals

Goal	Measurement	Deadline
Improve math grade by one letter grade	Exam scores, assignments, quizzes	End of semester
Complete a research project	Completion, quality of work	Mid-semester
Join an academic club	Attendance, participation	Next month

3. Create an Action Plan

Goal	Steps	Resources Needed
Improve math grade	1. Weekly tutoring sessions	Tutoring, practice tests
	2. Daily math homework	
	3. Review sessions with teacher	
Complete a research project	1. Select a topic	Research materials
	2. Conduct research	Library access
	3. Write and present project	Teacher guidance
Join an academic club	1. Research clubs	Club listings
	2. Attend meetings	School calendar
	3. Participate in activities	Transport

67. Define What Success Means to You

Success often gets portrayed in terms of money, fame, or status. But true success is completely personal—only you can define what it means for your life. Take time to get clear on what success looks like to you. Is it academic achievements, athletic accomplishments, artistic ventures, or making scientific discoveries? Or perhaps it's about starting a nonprofit, being an entrepreneur, having a vibrant social life, or dedicating yourself to a cause? There are no right or wrong answers.

Once you identify what success means to you, visualize it in vivid sensory detail. Picture yourself actively thriving and happy in this version of success. Write your vision down so you can reference and add to it whenever needed. Keep it posted somewhere you'll see it often as a reminder to stay focused on your unique priorities and what matters most to you. Let your definition of success guide your goals, decisions and next steps. Revisit it whenever challenges arise or when you're feeling lost—it will keep you aligned with your aspirations and motivate you to persevere. Remember, you get to shape your success on your terms!

68. Explore Different Career Interests

It can be a bit overwhelming to figure out what you want to do with your life when you are still so young, but there are things you can do to help point you in the right direction. Things like self-assessment of skills, interests, and values, researching different career paths and industries, and seeking guidance and mentorship for career exploration. After all, the best way to learn is working under the wings of people with first-hand experience. Don't forget that you can also talk to a guidance counselor or teacher, your parents, or your friends—they might help you figure out what you want to do.

69. Work Hard

Spoiler alert! There's no such thing as an overnight success. Anyone who's truly made it has put in years of hard work to reach their goals. Take Beyoncé and Taylor Swift for example. While other girls their age were going to parties and shopping at the mall, they were focused on honing their craft. Beyoncé spent hours every week rehearsing dance routines and vocal exercises. Taylor was writing songs and learning to play different musical instruments. They showed up day after day and poured passion into every lyric and performance. And look what they've achieved.

Tempting shortcuts may promise instant results, but real achievement comes through consistent effort over time. Whatever your goals—whether it's getting good grades, excelling in sport, or mastering a new hobby—requires hard work, patience, and perseverance. Stay focused on playing the long game, put in the effort, and you'll be rewarded.

70. Build Essential Skills

Essential skills are the foundation upon which all other skills are built, and they are critical to success in any aspect of life. Think of them like the building blocks of your journey, without which you wouldn't be able to achieve your goals or reach your full potential.

They include communication, problem-solving, critical thinking, teamwork, time management, and adaptability. These skills are not just beneficial in one specific area of your life, but are transferable and applicable to any situation or career path you might choose.

The great thing is, you don't need to do a course to learn them. For example, to work on communication, you can join a debate team or participate in group discussions. Or for problem-solving, solve puzzles, riddles, or brain teasers.

Look for opportunities in your daily life to practice and strengthen these essential skills—they will be invaluable as you pursue your dreams.

71. Build a Solid Resume

Kick starting your dreams often starts with getting your first job, which is where a solid resume comes in handy. Your resume is your personal marketing tool, showcasing your impressive skills, activities, and traits—even without paid work experience.

Here are some tips to help you craft a stand out resume that gets you noticed.

- List your academic achievements. This can include the honor roll, sports teams, clubs, and volunteer work. Be sure to detail any leadership roles within these, for example, planning events, leading a team, and managing projects.
- Talk about the skills you've gained from hobbies such as communication from blogging or collaboration from community theater.
- Highlight special talents like foreign languages, musical abilities, or coding skills. Let your unique personality and passions shine.
- Structure your resume clearly and cater it to each application. You can find ready-made templates online you can use.

Remember, a strong resume tells a story about you beyond school and jobs. It is often the first impression you give to a prospective employer, so put in the time and effort to make it the best it can be.

Be the Change

Making a Positive Impact in Your World

You are extraordinary. Within you exists an incredible power to impact the world in profound ways. You might not feel like you can truly make a difference at your age. But I'm here to tell you that the world needs your voice, passion, and energy more than ever.

Standing up for what you believe in, challenging injustices, and inspiring others through your actions is how change happens. This is how we build a better future for all.

Don't let anyone tell you you're too young to make a meaningful impact. History has shown time and again that young people can be the catalyst for momentous positive change. Look at Malala Yousafzai, who survived a gunshot at 15 years old and went on to become the youngest Nobel Peace Prize laureate for her advocacy of girls' education. Or Greta Thunberg, who sparked a global movement against climate change as a 15-year-old student holding solitary school strikes. Their voices reverberated across the globe.

The ripple effects of your actions, no matter how small, can be enormous. It starts with you deciding to show up, speak up, and take the lead. Are you ready to change the world?

72. Find Your Voice

Your voice can be a catalyst for change. It has the power to inspire, challenge, and provoke thought. Stand tall and speak your truth, even if your voice quivers with apprehension. Remember, it is often in moments of vulnerability that our voices resonate the loudest.

Look at poet Amanda Gorman, who courageously spoke at the presidential inauguration at just 22 years old. Or Gitanjali Rao, an American inventor and scientist known for her work in water contamination detection and cyberbullying prevention. In 2020, at age 15, Gitanjali was named TIME's first "Kid of the Year". These young women show that influential voices can emerge at any age.

Know too, that standing up for what matters need not be a solitary endeavor. Surround yourself with like-minded individuals who share your passion and values. Together, you can amplify your impact, support one another, and create a community that fosters courage and resilience.

Always remember, your unique voice is a gift—use it to speak your truth and touch people's hearts and minds.

73. Help Others

Using your skills to help others is not only a selfless act but also a rewarding experience. Whether it's sharing your knowledge, lending a helping hand, or using your talents for a greater cause, you have the power to make a positive impact. By offering your skills to those in need, you can bring joy, create change, and inspire others. Whether it's tutoring a classmate, volunteering at a local organization—more on that in a minute—or using your artistic abilities to raise awareness, your skills have the potential to make a difference in someone's life. So, embrace your abilities and find ways to use them to uplift others and contribute to a better world.

74. Volunteer in Your Local Community

I know you're busy with school, friends, and all your other commitments, but I want to encourage you, if you can, to make some time for volunteering. I know, I know—one more thing to add to your plate. But hear me out, volunteering can be so rewarding for you and for the people or causes you help out.

It's a great way to explore your interests and give back to your community. Whether you love animals, want to help the elderly, are into politics or the environment, there are so many ways for your passions to make a difference. You could volunteer at an animal shelter, bake cookies for a community bake sale, join a beach clean-up, or deliver meals to senior citizens.

Not only will volunteering allow you to practice important skills like leadership, empathy, and problem-solving, but you can also connect with like-minded people. And nothing beats that feel-good rush you get from knowing you've helped make someone's day a little brighter.

I promise, once you start, you'll be hooked. So find an issue you care about, do your research, and make volunteering a habit. The people and organizations you assist will be so grateful, and you'll gain perspective and experience that truly enrich your life. Now get out there and start changing the world!

75. Inspire Others Through Your Actions

Actions speak louder than words. Remember that even the smallest acts can have a significant impact. Whether it's signing a petition, writing a letter to a representative, or engaging in peaceful protests, every action counts. Embrace the power of collective action and celebrate the incremental change that comes from these seemingly insignificant gestures.

76. Take Care of the Planet

This earth is your one and only home, so you have to take care of it so that it can take care of you. One way you can make a positive impact is by being mindful of your choices, particularly when it comes to fast fashion. Fast fashion is characterized as cheaply made clothing produced at a rapid pace, which has a devastating impact on the environment. When you opt for sustainable fashion choices, such as buying secondhand or supporting ethical brands, you can help reduce waste and promote a more sustainable industry.

Small changes in your daily life can make a big difference. Reduce, reuse, and recycle whenever possible. Conserve energy by turning off lights and unplugging electronics when not in use. Plant trees, participate in community clean-ups, and educate others about the importance of environmental stewardship.

Remember, every action counts. By taking care of the planet, you are ensuring a healthier future for yourself and generations to come.

77. Engage With Politics

Our voices matter and voting is how we collectively shape our society. Even though you may not be old enough to vote yet, it's never too early to start educating yourself on political issues and candidates. That way, when the time comes to cast your first ballot, you'll be ready to make informed choices that align with your values.

Stay curious by reading reputable news sources across the ideological spectrum. Discuss hot topics respectfully during family dinners or with friends. Learn about how government works at the city, state, and national level. Do research on political parties and where they stand. Follow debates to understand differing views on the challenges we face as a nation. The more informed you are, the better equipped you'll be to thoughtfully evaluate candidates and causes.

While voting may seem far off, these teen years are when you start cementing your political beliefs. So, ask lots of questions, keep an open but critical mind, and determine what matters most to you. Our future is shaped by young engaged citizens like you!

Slay Your Schedule

Time-Saving Tips to Get More Done

Time is like that elusive friend who always seems to slip through our fingers. It's a mysterious force that can feel beyond our control. But guess what? It's also a super valuable resource that, when we master it, can unlock incredible productivity, personal growth, and a whole lot of fulfillment.

In today's crazy, fast-paced world, where distractions are everywhere and demands on our time never seem to end, mastering the art of time management is like having a secret superpower. It's all about making smart choices, setting goals, and using our precious time in a way that matches our dreams and values.

When we rock at time management, we can achieve way more in way less time, say goodbye to stress, and create balance in our lives. So, how do smart girls manage and make their time work for them? I've got just the tips for you.

78. Get Up Early

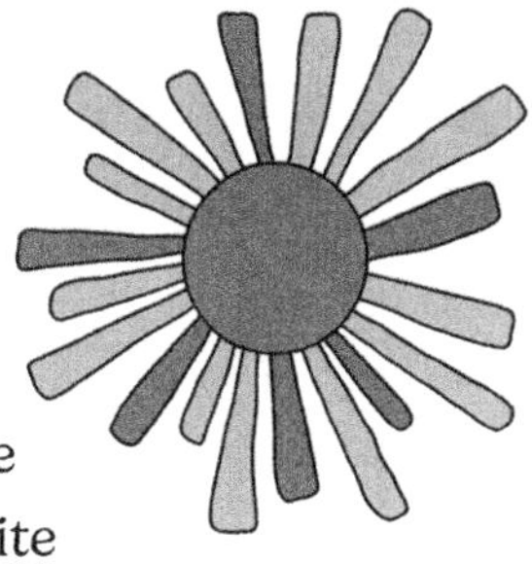

Rise and shine! Waking up early is a chance to start your day with intention, clarity, and a sense of calm. Those quiet moments before the world wakes up are precious. You can sip your tea or juice, write in your journal, do some yoga stretches, or just sit in meditation. Starting your day centered and calm so you're not rushed or stressed sets a positive tone. You'll have time for self-care and breakfast, so you can nourish your body and spirit.

Waking up early also lets you get a head start on your responsibilities. You can finish your homework, study for that test, or work on big projects without distraction. The early morning hours are perfect for deep focus and big-picture thinking before the busyness of the day sets in.

Being an early riser can make you feel deeply satisfied knowing you've accomplished so much before others are even out of bed! Having that quiet time to reflect and prepare also boosts your productivity all day long.

As an added bonus, early mornings are beautiful. Watching the sunrise and hearing the world come to life—it's a magical time that you miss out on if you're sleeping in. Waking up early helped me start loving mornings!

So, try it out for a week and see how you feel. Set that alarm clock a little earlier, embrace the tranquility of the early hours, and seize the day with enthusiasm. You'll be amazed at how waking up early can transform your life and help you make the most of every precious moment.

79. Be Organized

Being organized is certainly something that's going to help you get more clarity on where your time is going and how you can make much better choices when it comes to your time. Here are some tips that might help you get your A-Game on:

- **Create a dedicated workspace that inspires you.** Add some fun decorations, plants, or even a motivational quote to make it your own personal haven for productivity.
- **Turn your to-do list into a game.** Assign points to each task based on its importance or difficulty. Challenge yourself to earn high scores by completing the tasks efficiently. Celebrate your victories and reward yourself with a small treat or break.
- **Time travel with time blocking.** Use it to assign specific time slots for each task or activity throughout the day. It helps you stay focused and prevents you from getting overwhelmed.
- **Colorful calendar magic.** Make your calendar visually appealing and exciting. Assign different colors to different types of activities or events. For example, use green for work-related tasks, blue for personal appointments, and pink for fun activities. This way, your calendar becomes a vibrant visual representation of your life.
- **Embrace the power of Post-It notes!** Use colorful sticky notes to jot down important reminders, tasks, or ideas. Stick them on your computer screen, mirror, or any visible surface. It adds a touch of fun while keeping you organized.
- **Acknowledge and celebrate your small accomplishments along the way.** Treat yourself to something you enjoy, like a favorite snack or a short break. Even the tiniest achievements deserve recognition and can motivate you to keep going.

Remember, organization doesn't have to be boring! Embrace the process with enthusiasm and make it your own.

80. Prioritize, Prioritize, Prioritize!

Have you ever heard of the Pareto Principle? No? Perhaps you know it by its more common name—the 80/20 rule.

Let me give you a quick history lesson. The Pareto principle is named after Italian economist Vilfredo Pareto, who, in 1906, noticed that about 80% of Italy's land was owned by only 20% of the population. He discovered too that 20% of his fruit trees bore 80% of the fruit. He then carried out studies in other countries and found a similar pattern—a small portion of causes tended to produce a large portion of results.

In simple terms, the 80/20 rule says 80% of results come from 20% of effort. So how can you use this principle to help you prioritize tasks? Let me tell you:

- Start by making a master list of all the things you have to do, then identify the vital few items that will create the most value and progress if done first. For example, if you have 10 tasks on your to-do list, determine the top two task that will deliver the most results or greatest impact.
- Focus your best energy on starting that 20% before less urgent tasks. You'll gain momentum, feel productive, and get more done by strategically tackling the essentials.
- Regularly schedule your priorities and re-evaluate often, focusing on those that will have the most impact.

So, next time you're facing a long to-do list, try this game-changing approach to time management. It might be tempting to start with easy tasks, but spending effort on high-impact activities will make everything feel more doable. Trust me, you'll be amazed by what you can accomplish.

81. Get On With It

Does this scenario ring a bell? You're engrossed in the latest episode of your favorite series. Suddenly, your mom enters the room and asks you to take out the trash. With a nonchalant shrug, you respond, "Sure, I'll do it a little later." But as the day progresses, that "little later" turns into a never-ending cycle of delay, and the task keeps haunting you like a persistent ghost.

We've all been there, caught in the clutches of procrastination. It's like a sneaky creature that creeps into our lives, whispering promises of relaxation and putting off responsibilities until tomorrow. But here's the truth: Tomorrow never really comes. It's a perpetual cycle that keeps us stuck, preventing us from reaching our full potential and achieving our goals.

So, how do you break free from this habit and reclaim your productivity? It all starts with a shift in mindset. Instead of viewing tasks as burdensome chores, you reframe them as stepping stones toward your dreams. Whether it's completing homework, practicing a musical instrument, or doing research, every task holds the potential to bring you closer to your aspirations.

But here's the secret: Taking that first step is often the hardest part. It's so easy to get overwhelmed and succumb to distractions like scrolling through social media or binge-watching videos. We convince ourselves that we'll feel more motivated and energized to tackle the task later, but deep down, we know it's a trap.

The good news is you have the power to break free from this cycle. It starts with a simple decision to get on with it, to take action in the present moment. Remember, the longer you delay, the more time slips away and the more challenging the task seems to become. By embracing a proactive mindset, you regain control of your time and unleash your inner productivity ninjas.

But let's be real. We're not robots, and staying focused can be a struggle. That's why it's essential to find strategies that work for us individually.

Whether it's using time-management techniques like breaking tasks into smaller, manageable chunks, or creating a motivating workspace, we can discover the methods that resonate with our unique personalities.

Oh, and when you stumble, because you're only human, remember to practice self-compassion and learn from your setbacks instead of letting them derail you completely.

82. Foster Self-Discipline

Self-discipline is going to get you where motivation can't. While motivation can be fleeting, self-discipline is the steady force that keeps you on track toward your goals. Here are some small yet powerful ways you can cultivate more self-discipline:

- Find your inner superhero. Think of yourself as a superhero with incredible willpower. Create a superhero alter ego and visualize yourself embodying their traits. When faced with temptation or distractions, tap into your superhero persona and channel their discipline. Hey, if Beyoncé (aka Sasha Fierce) can do it, then so can you!
- Get yourself an accountability buddy, someone who shares your goals and can keep you in check. Set up regular check-ins or challenges together. Friendly competition and support can make staying disciplined more enjoyable.
- Design a reward system that aligns with your goals. Break down your journey into milestones and assign rewards for reaching each one. Treat yourself to something you love.
- Build rituals and routines. Start your day with activities that put you in the headspace for the day ahead. This helps create structure and discipline, setting you up for success.

Remember, building self-discipline is like training a muscle. It takes time, consistency, and a positive mindset.

83. Turn Up on Time

One of my friends used to be a flight attendant for an airline. She didn't have the luxury of arriving late to work; the pilots weren't going to hold the plane for her. Even now, many years later, when we make plans to catch up, I know she'll always be a few minutes early.

Now you might not have a flight to catch, but turning up when you say you will is important. Why? Because turning up on time shows the world that you value and respect both your own time and the time of others. It's a habit that will serve you well throughout life because it demonstrates reliability, professionalism, and a strong work ethic. It shows that you are organized, dependable, and committed to your responsibilities. Whether it's for school, work, or social engagements, arriving on time sets a positive impression and builds trust with others. Set those alarms, plan ahead, and make punctuality a priority.

Digital Diva

Navigating Tech and Social Media with Mindfulness

Imagine this: You're scrolling through your favorite social media platform, double-tapping those adorable puppy pictures, and basking in the glory of your friend's mouth-watering food posts. But wait, have you ever stopped to wonder how this digital realm affects our minds, hearts, and overall well-being?

We live in a world where technology is both our best friend and our mischievous frenemy. It connects us, entertains us, and empowers us, but it can also suck us into a vortex of mindless scrolling and comparison traps. But don't worry, this chapter will equip you with the art of mindful tech navigation—a superpower that will transform you into the ultimate digital diva!

With a few savvy and helpful tips, we're going to explore the wondrous landscapes of social media and learn how to strike the perfect balance between screen time and self-care. So, put on your virtual thinking caps and get ready to ride the waves of this awe-inspiring digital adventure!

84. Regulate Your Social Media Use

I love spending a little time on social media. I mean, who doesn't love a good ol' Tik-Tok video or some funny cat reel? But the one thing I do understand is that there needs to be boundaries in place. Here are some handy tips on regulating your social media usage:

- Set a time limit for social media, so you can actually have a life outside the virtual world. Trust me, the real world has better resolution!
- Avoid the comparison trap by remembering that people only post their highlight reels on social media. So, instead of feeling FOMO (Fear of Missing Out), embrace JOMO (Joy of Missing Out) and enjoy your own unique journey. Turn off those notifications. You don't need your phone buzzing every time someone likes your post.
- Create a "no-phone zone" during meals. Trust me, your food will taste better when you're not busy taking pictures of it. Plus, your dining companions might appreciate some actual conversation.
- When you feel the urge to mindlessly scroll, try a new hobby instead. Writing or painting can be more rewarding than endless cat videos.

85. Stay Safe Online

Social media has become our ultimate playground for connection and self-expression. But before you immerse yourself into the virtual world, we need to talk about staying safe online so that you can have a fun-filled social media experience that's free from any online dangers.

Here are a few things I want you to remember about navigating your virtual world:

- Treat your passwords like your underwear—change them regularly, and don't share them with anyone!
- Scammers are pretty sophisticated these days, and your best protection from being scammed is to arm yourself with knowledge of common red flags. Be wary of emails that seem too good to be true, have poor spelling or grammar, or come from an unknown sender. Your Spidey Senses should kick in if an email creates a false sense of urgency, threatens dire consequences, or promises unbelievable prizes. Avoid clicking links or opening attachments in scam emails, as they may contain malware. Before providing any information or money, verify the source by calling the company directly. And don't forget the age old saying—if it sounds too good to be true, it probably is.
- Keep your privacy settings on lockdown! Don't let strangers peek into your personal life like nosy neighbors. Adjust your settings so only friends can see your posts, pics, and info. And even then, remember that everything online can spread widely and stick around forever. So share thoughtfully and keep personal details limited. You get to choose who sees your business!
- Backup your important files regularly. All your essays, photos, videos—save copies in multiple places. Store them on an external hard drive and in the cloud. That way, if your computer crashes, you won't have to start totally from scratch.

86. Think Twice Before Posting

In the age of social media, it can be tempting to want to share every aspect of your life. With just a few taps on your device, you can instantly broadcast your photos, thoughts, experiences, and emotions to a global audience.

While social media can offer lots of benefits like staying connected with friends and expressing creativity, it's essential to exercise caution and think twice before hitting that 'post' button. Here are some things to keep in mind.

- Remember, what happens on the Internet stays on the Internet... forever! Before you post that embarrassing party pic, ask yourself, do I want a future friend, partner, or employer to see it? If the answer is no, then put your phone away.
- Avoid sharing overly personal or sensitive images. You don't want your private moments to become public spectacles. Keep it classy.
- When in doubt, consider the grandma test. If you wouldn't want your grandma to see the image, it's probably best not to share it.
- Be mindful of the background in your photos. You don't want unintended surprises lurking behind you. No one needs to see your messy room or your pet doing something... inappropriate.
- Respect others' privacy by asking for permission before posting their pictures. Not everyone wants to be an Internet sensation.

Remember, the Internet has a long memory, so it's important to always think twice before you share.

87. Upgrade Your Digital Skills

Technology is changing so quickly that staying up-to-date with the latest digital skills is not only beneficial in the now but will also set you up for success in the future. While you don't have to become a coding expert, being familiar with emerging technologies like Artificial Intelligence (AI) will give you a competitive edge. Understanding the basics of AI can open doors to various fields, from healthcare to marketing.

In today's digital age, visual content is king, and being able to create and edit videos can enhance your communication abilities and creative expression. Whether it's for school projects, personal vlogs, or future career endeavors, video editing skills can be a valuable asset.

By upgrading your digital skills, you are equipping yourself with tools that can enhance your productivity, creativity, and problem-solving abilities. Embrace the ever-evolving digital landscape, explore online resources, take advantage of tutorials and courses, and stay curious about the latest advancements.

Remember, investing in your digital skills now can pay off in the long run, opening doors to exciting opportunities and helping you thrive in a technology-driven world.

Life Hacks

Essential Skills for Independence

We're almost at the very last chapter, can you believe that we made it this far? And in case you're worried about it being very long, this is going to be relatively short and sweet. What I do want to do, though, is share a couple of life hacks that will get you far in life; life hacks that will make your life slightly easier. Now I know that a life hack is not going to necessarily help you win some grand prize, but hey, who needs a Nobel Peace Prize when you have the power to make your everyday life a little easier?

Life hacks are like secret weapons in your arsenal, ready to tackle those tiny little problems that pop up when you least expect them. Think of them as your personal cheat codes for navigating the ups and downs of life and strategies that will help you along the way as you go out to navigate the great big world on your own.

So, let's dive in, and remember this while you're at it: The simplest tricks can lead to the biggest victories. Here are a few of my favorite tips that will ensure that you not only survive but thrive in life!

88. Make Your Bed

Making your bed in the morning is like giving a high-five to the day ahead. It sets the tone for productivity and tells the universe, "Hey, I've got my act together!" Plus, there's something oddly satisfying about smoothing out those sheets and fluffing those pillows. It's like a mini victory before you even leave the bedroom. So allow yourself to conquer the day, one tucked corner at a time!

89. Learn How to Cook

Cooking is more than just a chore or a means to satisfy your hunger—it's a life skill that can bring you joy, independence, and a whole lot of deliciousness.

First off, it opens up a world of culinary possibilities. No longer will you be limited to pre-packaged meals or takeout. By mastering a few basic cooking techniques, you can whip up a wide range of dishes, from simple and comforting to gourmet and impressive. Imagine the satisfaction of creating a mouthwatering meal from scratch and sharing it with your loved ones.

Cooking also gives you the power to take control of your health. When you cook your own meals, you have full control over the ingredients, portion sizes, and cooking methods. You can choose fresh, wholesome ingredients and experiment with different flavors and cuisines.

Let's not forget about the financial benefits of cooking. Eating out or ordering takeout can be so expensive, especially if it becomes a regular habit. If you cook at home, however, you can save a significant amount of money.

Lastly, it is a valuable life skill that will serve you well throughout your life. Whether you're living on your own, hosting a dinner party, or simply wanting to impress your future roommates, having cooking skills under your belt will make you more self-sufficient and confident in the kitchen.

Here are some handy tips that you can keep in mind as you embark on a culinary adventure of your own:

- Start with easy-to-follow recipes that have fewer ingredients and basic cooking techniques. This will help you build confidence and gradually expand your skills.
- When starting out, it's best to follow recipes closely. Pay attention to measurements, cooking times, and instructions. As you gain experience, you can start experimenting and adding your own twists.
- Don't be afraid to make mistakes in the kitchen. It's all part of the learning process. Learn from them, adapt, and keep trying. Even professional chefs make mistakes!
- Cooking can be a fun and social activity. Invite friends or family members to join you in the kitchen. You can learn from each other, share tips, and enjoy the process together.
- Online platforms like YouTube are filled with cooking tutorials and demonstrations. Watch videos from reputable chefs or cooking channels to learn new techniques and get inspired.
- Like any skill, cooking improves with practice. Don't get discouraged if a dish doesn't turn out perfectly the first time. Keep practicing, experimenting, and enjoying the journey of becoming a skilled cook.

Happy cooking!

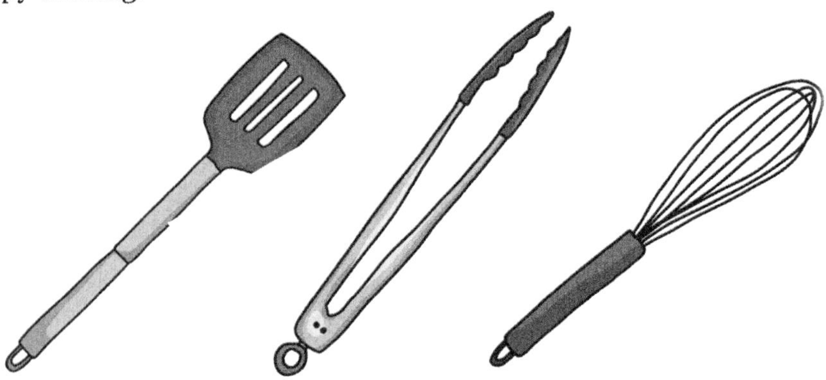

90. Clean Up After Yourself

No one likes a slob. Sure, cleaning might not be how you want to spend your spare time, but a clean and organized environment can make you feel like you've got your life together.

Here's a pro tip I picked up from my days in the fast-food trenches: clean as you go. Don't let things accumulate into a chaotic avalanche of mess. By tackling the tidying task bit by bit, you keep the cleanup effort to a minimum.

Trust me, your future room-mates will thank you for it!

91. Learn to Manage Your Money

Learning to budget and manage money is what will help you make smarter financial decisions and avoid those awkward moments when you're short on cash. By setting limits and tracking your expenses, you'll have a better handle on your money and be able to save up for the things that matter most to you.

There's something else I want you to remember: Budgeting isn't just about saying "no" to spending. It's also about saying "yes" to your goals and dreams. Want to save up for that dream vacation? Or maybe you're eyeing that shiny new gadget? Budgeting will help you allocate money toward your goals and watch your savings grow. It's like having your own personal money tree.

Now, I get it. Budgeting can feel overwhelming, especially when you're just starting out, but there are plenty of resources out there to help you. From budgeting apps to online tutorials, there's something for everyone. And hey, you can even turn it into a fun challenge with your friends. Who can save the most money in a month?

92. Get a Part-Time Job

If you want to level-up your skills, gain some independence, and earn some extra cash, getting a part-time job is a no-brainer.

First and foremost, it is a fantastic opportunity for you to develop valuable skills that will serve you well in the future. Whether it's customer service, time management, teamwork, or problem-solving, every job comes with its own set of skills to learn and master. These skills will not only boost your resume but also make you stand out from the crowd when applying for college or future career opportunities.

Oh, and speaking of resumes, having a part-time job shows your future employers that you're responsible, reliable, and capable of juggling multiple commitments. It demonstrates your work ethic and dedication, which are qualities that are highly valued in any professional setting. Plus, you'll have real-life examples to share during interviews, making you a more compelling candidate.

Let's not forget about the financial perks. A part-time job means having your own source of income. You'll have the power to save up for those jeans or dresses you have been eyeing, save for a car, or simply have some spending money for fun activities with friends. Learning to manage your finances at an early age is a valuable skill that will set you up for success in the long run.

But it's not all about the money. You also get a sense of independence and confidence. You'll learn how to navigate the professional world, interact with different types of people, and handle responsibilities on your own. It's a stepping stone toward adulthood and a chance to discover your strengths and passions.

Lastly, let's not forget the social aspect. You'll meet new people, make friends, and expand your network. These connections can be invaluable for future opportunities, mentorship, or even lifelong friendships. So get on out there and embrace the world of work and the opportunities that are available to you!

93. Do Your Laundry

Laundry, oh, laundry... the never-ending cycle of clean clothes to dirty clothes. But you know what else doing laundry does? It saves us from the dreaded "I have nothing to wear" crisis.

Doing your laundry is not just about independence but also about maintaining cleanliness and hygiene. Wearing clean clothes not only feels great but also keeps you fresh and confident.

Now, doing laundry may seem daunting at first, but it's actually a straightforward process that anyone can master. And, the more you do it, the more confident and efficient you'll become.

Here are a few final hacks to help you get through the process with ease:

- Start by separating your clothes into different piles based on color and fabric type.
- Read the labels on your clothes to determine the appropriate washing and drying settings. Following the manufacturer's instructions will help prolong the life of your garments.
- Cold water is often sufficient for cleaning most clothes, and it helps save energy. Reserve hot water for heavily soiled items or bedding.
- Follow the recommended amount of detergent for each load, but don't be tempted to use more than necessary. Excess detergent can leave residue on your clothes and even cause skin irritation.
- To quickly remove lint or pet hair from your clothes, use a lint roller or wrap some tape around your hand with the sticky side facing out.
- Folding your clothes right after they come out of the dryer helps prevent wrinkles and keeps your wardrobe organized. Plus, it saves you from having to iron later.

94. Practice Personal Safety

As a young woman, you've got to know how to take care of yourself because (and the intention here is not to scare you) there are dangers lurking out there. But don't worry, I've got some tips to help keep you safe.

First things first, trust your gut instincts. If something feels off, don't hesitate to make a quick exit. Stay aware of your surroundings, especially when you're exploring new places or strutting your stuff solo. It's always smart to have a buddy system in place and let someone know where you're going.

Learning a few basic self-defence techniques can boost your confidence, and it's also a great excuse to unleash your inner ninja!

You also want to make sure that you keep those emergency numbers on speed dial and have a plan in case of any unexpected situations. And remember, safety is all about being prepared, staying aware, and having each other's backs.

So have fun, be fabulous, and enjoy yourself when you're out and about, but don't forget to put safety at the forefront.

95. Learn How to Drive

Learning to drive isn't just about memorizing the road rules and conquering the mechanics of a car; it's about gaining independence, confidence, and control over your own journey. It opens up a world of possibilities, from impromptu road trips to being the designated driver for your squad.

So, if the opportunity to learn to drive comes your way, grab it with both hands. Consider it a skill set that goes beyond the road, empowering you personally and setting you up for whatever life throws your way. Embrace the challenges, enjoy the ride, and soon you'll be navigating the twists and turns of life with a smile and a full tank of gas.

96. Learn How to Swim

Now, I bet you that you didn't expect to find this life hack in here, now did you? But alas, here it is.

Being able to swim improves your physical fitness, coordination, and mental strength. It's also an essential safety skill. You never know when you might need to react quickly to help yourself or others in the water. Knowing how to swim could save your life or someone else's.

Beyond safety, swimming opens up so many fun opportunities, too! You can enjoy pool parties with friends, try out for the swim team, or just get a great workout swimming laps. It feels incredible to move through the water with confidence and grace.

So don't wait any longer to learn this essential skill. Swimming lessons are fun and teach lifesaving techniques like floating, treading water, and efficient strokes. Hit the pool today! I promise you won't regret it. The sense of freedom and power you'll gain in the water is priceless.

97. Mind Your Manners

I know we've already talked about saying thank you, but don't forget other ways you can show good manners; by saying please, addressing people correctly, opening doors, and so forth. That simple "please" can go a long way in showing respect and consideration for others. Manners also go beyond just words and actions. It's about being mindful of how our behavior affects others and treating everyone with kindness and empathy. So, make good manners a part of your daily life and create a world where respect and courtesy reign supreme.

98. Start a Side Hustle

When I was young, a side hustle was as sophisticated as babysitting or a lemonade stand on the street corner. Today, there are so many more opportunities for smart girls with an entrepreneurial spirit. Whether it's selling handmade crafts, offering tutoring services, or starting an online store, a side hustle can be a creative outlet and a way to earn some extra cash. It's a chance to explore your passions, develop new skills, and gain valuable experience.

Remember, starting small is okay, and with dedication and perseverance, your side hustle might just turn into something amazing.

99. Grocery Shop Like a Pro

Grocery shopping may seem like a mundane chore, but it's such an important life skill for teens to start practicing... unless you want to spend your life eating beans on toast!

Here are some tips to get you started:

- **Make a shopping list.** Plan your meals for the week and create a list of the ingredients you need. Stick to the list to avoid unnecessary purchases.
- **Eat before you go.** Shopping on an empty stomach can lead to impulse buys.
- **Choose whole foods.** Opt for fresh fruits, vegetables, whole grains, and lean proteins. These items are generally healthier than processed foods.
- **Shop the perimeter.** The perimeter of the store usually contains fresh produce, dairy, and proteins. Focus on these areas for healthier options.
- **Compare unit prices.** Check the unit price (price per ounce or pound) to determine the best value for your money.
- **Be mindful of expiration dates.** Nobody likes sour milk! Check expiration dates on perishable items to ensure freshness.
- **Bring reusable bags.** Save on plastic bags by bringing your own reusable bags. Some stores may even offer discounts for using your own bags.
- **Buy seasonal produce.** Seasonal fruits and vegetables are usually fresher and more affordable. Check what's in season and plan meals around those items.

By incorporating these tips, you'll be grocery shopping like a pro in no time.

100. Be Prepared

Growing up, my older brother was a Boy Scout. I always remembered their motto, "Be Prepared." It applies just as much to us girls! As a teen, you need to know how to handle crisis situations on your own. While scary to think about, taking simple steps now will give you the confidence and ability to react quickly and potentially save lives. Here are a few ideas:

- Have an emergency kit in your locker or backpack with bandages, antiseptic wipes, medication if needed, flashlight, backup phone charger and some food like energy bars. This can help you assist with injuries, provide light if the power goes out, and keep you nourished if stuck somewhere for hours.
- Learn basic first aid like CPR, stopping bleeding, treating sprains, and responding to allergic reactions, which are common emergencies. Take free online classes to get trained. Always know where fire alarms and exits are in public places.
- Have a plan for getting home if you're unable to drive, get a lift, or if public transportation shuts down. Share your location on your phone when commuting or out at night. Avoid walking alone in isolated areas. Carry yourself confidently and be alert to your surroundings.

Life is full of unexpected curve balls, so staying vigilant, having a plan just in case things go wrong, and trusting your instincts can help keep you safe in difficult and unpredictable situations.

One Last Thing...

You're going to be okay! Believe me, you are. This rollercoaster ride called teenagehood is full of wild surprises, like pop quizzes on Mondays and sudden prom dress emergencies. There will definitely be days when you feel like screaming into your pillow out of sheer frustration—and that's okay. We've all been there!

But amidst the chaos, don't forget to embrace your cleverness, lightheartedness, and relatability. Remember that laughter is the best medicine, and a good sense of humor can help you navigate even the stickiest of situations. You never know when you'll need to whip out a quick joke to diffuse tension or make new friends at the lunch table.

We've explored 100 empowering things that smart girls do to conquer the teenage world with style. From embracing who you are to navigating friendships and rocking the body you have, you've gained a treasure trove of knowledge.

But before we say our goodbyes, let me share with you a few things to put a smile on your face when things get a little tough:

- When life gives you lemons, forget lemonade—make a lemon meringue pie and share it with your loved ones.
- Remember that it's okay to have a bad hair day or wear mismatched socks—imperfections make us human, and that's what makes us beautiful.
- Never underestimate the power of a good joke. It might not solve world problems, but it can certainly lighten the mood.

Before we wrap things up, here is one final piece of advice for you.

101. Remember you are capable of achieving big, bold, brilliant things and making a positive impact in this world.

Don't ever let anyone bring you down. Always have the courage to believe in yourself and your dreams and, most importantly, don't ever stop fighting for them.

As you close this book, go forth with laughter in your heart and a twinkle in your eye. You have all the ingredients to conquer the world, armed with the power of smart decisions, relentless determination, and a good sense of humor.

Keep being smart, keep thriving, and keep achieving. And remember, when life gets tough, a well-timed giggle can sometimes be the best solution.

You've got this! Stay fabulous!

About the Author

Rachel Spade is an author and business consultant with over 20 years of experience helping individuals, teams, and organizations to drive behavioral and transformational change.

She is a passionate advocate for personal development and self-improvement. She believes that everyone has the potential to grow and achieve their goals, and she is dedicated to helping people tap into their potential and make positive changes in their lives.

In *101 Things Smart Girls Do*, Rachel gives practical guidance and tips to young teenage girls to help them become the fearless, resilient, and unstoppable young women they are destined to be.

With her unique blend of expertise and compassion, Rachel is committed to helping people create the lives they want and to becoming the best versions of themselves.

Rachel holds a degree in social science and has a background in publishing, journalism, change management, and communications.

References

A Sweet Life. (2020, December 14). *How to embrace your individuality—how to be unique.* ASweatLife. https://asweatlife.com/2020/12/6-ways-to-embrace-your-individuality/

Alonto-Younes, S (2022, April 5). *How Vera Wang's Biggest Failure Led to Her Fashion Empire.* https://www.linkedin.com/pulse/how-vera-wangs-biggest-failure-led-her-fashion-empire-alonto-younes/

Batterham, A. (2020, May 16). *How to be your own cheerleader.* Medium. https://audrey-batterham.medium.com/how-to-be-your-own-cheerleader-a68657726329

Bonner, J. (2021, June 24). *Do you embrace your individuality?* www.linkedin.com. https://www.linkedin.com/pulse/do-you-embrace-your-individuality-james-bonner

Bucloh, L. (2018). *5 Ways to know your feelings better* (for Teens). KidsHealth. Kidshealth.org. https://kidshealth.org/en/teens/emotional-awareness.html

Busch, B. (2017, November 3). *Emotional intelligence: why it matters and how to teach it.* The Guardian. https://www.theguardian.com/teacher-network/2017/nov/03/emotional-intelligence-why-it-matters-and-how-to-teach-it

Carpenter, T. (2023, March 27). *Sara Blakely: Celebrating Failure and Redefining Business Culture.* Strixus, https://strixus.com/entry/sara-blakely-celebrating-failure-and-redefining-business-culture-18138#

Cherry, K. (2017). *Understanding body language and facial expressions.* Verywell well. https://www.verywellmind.com/understand-body-language-and-facial-expressions-4147228

Clausing, G. (2020, February 7). *Why you should watch your words.* IMOM. https://www.imom.com/watch-your-words/

Conlon, C. (2014, March 5). *40 Simple ways to practice gratitude.* Lifehack. https://www.lifehack.org/articles/communication/40-simple-ways-practice-gratitude.html

DiLeone, M. (2016, June 27). *How to let go of negative, limiting beliefs about yourself.* Tiny Buddha. https://tinybuddha.com/blog/how-let-go-negative-limiting-beliefs-about-yourself/

Duggal, N. (2018, July 13). *Emotional intelligence in the workplace: why you need it, how to get it.* Simplilearn.com; Simplilearn. https://www.simplilearn.com/emotional-intelligence-what-why-and-how-article

Gonzalves, K. (2015, March 11). *20 Small ways to start loving your body, even When It's Hard.* Mindbodygreen. https://www.mindbodygreen.com/articles/how-to-love-your-body

Greene, N. (2021, May 13). *Dealing with teen emotions.* Psych Central. https://psychcentral.com/blog/techniques-for-teens-how-to-cope-with-your-emotions

Gupta, S. (2021, March 21). *What does the saying "Don't sweat the small stuff" mean?* Verywell well. https://www.verywellmind.com/what-does-the-saying-dont-sweat-the-small-stuff-mean-5224156

Johnson, E. B. (2019, March 19). *Why learning to love my body is the hardest thing I've ever done.* Practical Growth. https://medium.com/practical-growth/learning-to-love-my-body-a25a3ea471bc

Lamothe, C. (2018, June 22). *The benefits of laughing at yourself, according to science.* Shondaland. https://www.shondaland.com/live/a21755063/benefits-laughing-at-yourself-self-deprecation-science-psychology/

Laoyan, S (2022, December 8) *Understanding the Pareto principle (The 80/20 rule).* https://asana.com/resources/pareto-principle-80-20-rule

Leech, J. (2022, January 6). *10 reasons why good sleep is important.* Healthline. https://www.healthline.com/nutrition/10-reasons-why-good-sleep-is-important

Leonard, K., & Watts, R. (2021, November 29). *The ultimate guide To S.M.A.R.T. Goals.* Forbes Advisor; Forbes. https://www.forbes.com/advisor/business/smart-goals/

LifeHack. (2013, February 26). *100 Incredible life hacks that make life so much easier.* Lifehack. https://www.lifehack.org/articles/lifestyle/100-life-hacks-that-make-life-easier.html

Lyness, D. (2019). *5 Ways to Prevent Stress Buildup (for Teens) - KidsHealth.* Kidshealth.org. https://kidshealth.org/en/teens/stress-tips.html

Mairanz, A. (2018, October 25). *The road to a positive mindset: be Your Own Cheerleader.* Empower Your Mind Therapy. https://eymtherapy.com/blog/positive-mindset-be-your-own-cheerleader/

Medical GPS. (n.d.). *Three best practices for showing empathy and compassion in healthcare.* https://blog.medicalgps.com/three-best-practices-for-showing-empathy-and-compassion-in-healthcare/#:~:text=Body%20 language%20makes%20the%20difference

Mental Health First Aid. (2019, June 26). *Five tips to help teens cope with stress.* Mental Health First Aid. https://www.mentalhealthfirstaid.org/2019/06/five-tips-to-help-teens-cope-with-stress/

Miles, M. (2022, July 20). *How to be a better friend: 10 Ways to up your friendship Game.* Betterup https://www.betterup.com/blog/how-to-be-a-better-friend

Monae, A. (2023, January 31). *Why you need to become your own cheerleader.* Entrepreneur. https://www.entrepreneur.com/living/why-you-need-to-become-your-own-cheerleader/442979#:~:text=In%20conclusion%2C%20being%20your%20own

Network, T. L. (2022, October 13). *Teenagers share their best life hacks.* The New York Times. https://www.nytimes.com/2022/10/13/learning/teenagers-share-their-best-life-hacks.html

Parker-Pope, T. (2019, October 28). *How to Be a Better Friend. New York Times.* https://www.nytimes.com/guides/smarterliving/how-to-be-a-better-friend

Prashad, A. (2015, November 28). *8 Steps for embracing your uniqueness* - Dr. Asha Prasad. https://drashaprasad.com/self-awareness/embrace-your-uniqueness/

Rebecca. (2021, January 6). *Dare to be different: 10 Ways to embrace your uniqueness.* Minimalism Made Simple. https://www.minimalismmadesimple.com/home/dare-to-be-different/

Rebecca. (2022, July 3). *15 Ways to Let go of Limiting Beliefs. Minimalism Made Simple.* https://www.minimalismmadesimple.com/home/limiting-beliefs/#:~:text=By%20repeating%20affirmations%2C%20you%20can

Robbins, M. (2010, June 7). *Be Your Own Cheerleader.* HuffPost. https://www.huffpost.com/entry/be-your-own-cheerleader_b_601496

Rowling, J.K. (n.d) *My Story.* https://stories.jkrowling.com/my-story/

Shortsleeve, C. (2022, October 13). *Asking for Help Is So Damn Hard. Here's How to Make It Easier.* Self. https://www.self.com/story/how-to-ask-for-help

Shubham, B (n.d.) *BRAIGO and my quest to make an advanced, affordable Braille printer.* https://sowc2015.unicef.org/stories/young-inventor-makes-lego-braille-printer/

Sorenson, D. (n.d.). *How to ask for help. Psyche Guides.* Psyche https://psyche.co/guides/how-to-ask-for-help-without-discomfort-or-apology

Sreenlvasen, S. (2021, April 5). *How Laughing at Yourself Can Be Good for Your Well-Being* | Psychology Today South Africa. Psychologytoday https://www.psychologytoday.com/za/blog/emotional-nourishment/202104/how-laughing-yourself-can-be-good-your-well-being

Telloian, C. (2022, January 27). *It's ok to be sad: 6 Reasons and how to manage sadness.* Psych Central. https://psychcentral.com/health/why-feeling-sad-is-actually-good

Udavant (Luna), S. (2022, July 25). *How to Overcome Loneliness And Enjoy Your Own Company.* Ascent Publication. https://medium.com/the-ascent/how-to-overcome-loneliness-and-enjoy-your-own-company-32aa48b7ac93

United States Patent and Trademark Office, (n.d.) *One girl's commitment.* https://www.uspto.gov/learning-and-resources/journeys-innovation/field-stories/one-girls-commitment

University of Minnesota. (n.d.). *10 Ways to be a more thankful person. Taking Charge of Your Health & Wellbeing.* https://www.takingcharge.csh.umn.edu/10-ways-be-more-thankful-person

Waters, S. (2021, September 20). *How to read body language and gain deeper emotional awareness.* Betterup.https://www.betterup.com/blog/how-to-read-body-language

WomensMedia. (2016, July 8). *8 Ways To Have More Gratitude Every Day.* Forbes. https://www.forbes.com/sites/womensmedia/2016/07/08/8-ways-to-have-more-gratitude-every-day/?sh=1e79aaf91d54

Wooll, M. (2022, November 11). *How to hold yourself accountable: 5 Tips.* Betterup https://www.betterup.com/blog/how-to-hold-yourself-accountable#:~:text=Self%2Daccountability%20means%20taking%20responsibility

Yadav, K. (2017, June 23). *Why you should watch your words.* Medium. https://medium.com/@kunalyadav/why-you-should-watch-your-words-16ceeb222377#:~:text=This%20is%20important%20because%20when

Zolli Candy (n.d.) *Our Story.* https://shop.zollipops.com/pages/our-story

Printed in Great Britain
by Amazon

56931124R00086